SHIPPING ONLY

ERIC AND US

'We shall remember, when our hair is white,
These clouded days revealed in radiant light.'

Drawing by Edward Ardizzone for the sonnet by Eric Blair
written in January 1919

Jacintha Buddicom

ERIC AND US
A Remembrance of
George Orwell

'When I sit down to write a book I do not say to myself "I am going to produce a work of art". I write it because there is some lie I want to expose, some fact to which I want to draw attention, and my initial concern is to get a hearing.'

George Orwell
– *Why I Write*, 1947

Leslie Frewin of London

First published 1974 by

Leslie Frewin Publishers Limited,
Five Goodwin's Court,
Saint Martin's Lane,
London WC2N 4LL, England.

Designed by Craig Dodd

This book is set in Linotype Pilgrim

Printed by the Compton Press, Compton Chamberlayne, Salisbury, Wiltshire, England.

Bound by Redwood Burn Ltd., Esher, Surrey.

ISBN 0 85632 0765

Dedication

To The Little Ones of yesterday
Eric's sister *Avril* and my sister *Guiny*
because we shared the past :

and to those young men of today,
my godson *Nicholas* and his brother *Chris*
because we believe in the future :

perhaps partly due to George Orwell –

There's Always Tomorrow

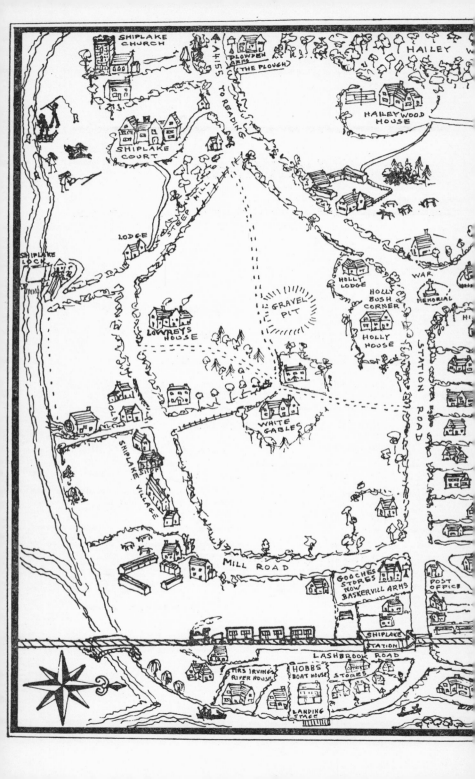

Acknowledgments

FIRST, MY GRATEFUL thanks to those who have given me active help. In alphabetical order:

To Ian Angus, keeper of the *Orwell Archive* at the University College London Library, for his encouragement and for arranging the photographic reproduction of my family's relics of Eric. Some of our snapshots were so faded that Mr Hitchcock should be specially congratulated on his excellent results. To Edward Ardizzone for his felicitous kindness in providing the frontispiece: a most happy picture of our contemporary youth. To Avril Blair – Eric's sister, now Mrs Dunn – for reading the manuscript and vetting it for authenticity; and also for reminding me of incidents I had forgotten, and giving information about the Blair Family Tree which I had not known before. To Cyril Connolly for the valuable quotation from his *Such Were the Joys* in the *New York Times Book Review* of 12 November 1972 and for other contemporary corroborative details.

Second, while many of the photographs reproduced are my own, some belong to my sister and the two of the 'Ticklerton

Shooting Party' were inherited by my niece; so thank you to Guinever Buddicom and Jennifer Buddicom – now Mrs Simon Brown – for lending them. Thanks also, to Messrs Giddy & Giddy of Henley-on-Thames for the photograph of 36 St Marks Road; and to Mrs Trudy Wilson for her photo of Rose Lawn, where she now resides.

Third, my gratitude to those publishers and owners of copyright who have allowed me to make various quotations: To Coles Publishing Company Ltd of Canada for the quotation from *Orwell: Animal Farm Notes* by Howard Fink. To Constable Publishers, together with the authors, Peter Stansky and William Abrahams for quotations from *The Unknown Orwell*. To Heinemann Educational Books Ltd for the quotation from *George Orwell: Selected Writings* edited by George Bott. To Macmillan Publishers and to David Higham Associates on behalf of the literary heirs of Miss Edith Sitwell, for the quotation from 'Heart and Mind', in *Song of the Cold*.

Two other authors, presumably by now no longer with us, I have not been able to trace. But I would offer acknowledgment to their literary heirs in the hope that they would be glad for these poems to give as much pleasure to others as they have given to me. 'The Clouds Were Tangled in the Trees' was definitely published, as I read it in some novel. I do not know whether the 'Sea Piece' and 'Rouen' by Fred Salusbury were ever published, but he certainly wrote them down for me.

J.B.

Contents

List of Illustrations

FRONTISPIECE
'We shall remember, when our hair is white,
These clouded days revealed in radiant light.'

Drawing by Edward Ardizzone

Between pages 138 and 139

1: THE SECOND-BIRTHDAY-PARTY BABY: Jacintha 1903.

Portrait by Richard Speaight

2: EDWARDIAN FAMILY: The Buddicom children Christmas 1907. *By Marshall, Henley-on-Thames*

3: HOLIDAY AT NEWQUAY: August 1908. *Snapshot by RAB*

4: TEAPARTY ON THE RIVER: July 1914. *By Noel Burke*

5: OUTSIDE THE FRONT DOOR AT TICKLERTON: about 1913 or 1914. *Snapshot by Lilian Buddicom*

6: HAY-WAIN AT CHARLTON HILL: September 1914.

Snapshot by Lilian Buddicom

7: THE WREKIN FROM CHARLTON HILL: 8th September 1914. *Snapshot by Lilian Buddicom*

8: THE CARRIAGE WAITING TO TAKE US TO CHURCH: CHARLTON HILL 1914. *Snapshot by Prosper*

9: ANOTHER PROBLEM CHILD: about 1914 or 1915.

xiv

Requiem for George Orwell

AVE ATQUE VALE

25 June 1903 – *23 January* 1950 – 1984

Hail and Farewell
To youth and lost companion
His funeral knell
Woke Freedom long ago :
No force can quail
The ultimate Britannian
Though winds of Hell
Through other deserts blow.
But how can brave young hopes such wastes foretell
Until
The shadows chill ?
Hail and Farewell.

Farewell. And Hail
To those who walk hereafter
His blazing trail
The rock-firm path he trod.
Of what avail
Is life bereft of laughter
O Infidel ?
The Innocence of God
Beset – betrayed – bedevilled – does not fail :
Man still
Has heart and will.
Farewell – and Hail.

Foreword

THE LAST WILL and testament of George Orwell was drawn up on 18 January 1950, three days before his death. It requested that no biography of him be written, and he signed it *Eric Blair*. On his tombstone in the churchyard at Sutton Courtenay is the legend :

Here Lies
Eric Arthur Blair
Born June 25th 1903
Died January 21st 1950

as he himself chose that it should be so inscribed.

It is possible that he prohibited biography because he thought nobody knew him well enough to write about him. But the embargo is now, it seems of necessity, lifted : so many books on George Orwell have already been published, and if they are not biographies, what are they? It has sometimes been a temptation to offer a few solid facts in place of the miasma of theories regarding his early years, deduced – with whatever enthusiasm and literary talent – by writers who were often mere children when he died, and who had never met him.

I never met George Orwell myself, though we had a brief correspondence early in 1949. But when we were youthful contemporaries I knew *Eric Blair* very well indeed. And through the ravelled overcoat covering Orwell, the golden armour of the quixotic young Eric still gleams brightly.

It was as Eric Blair he was born : it was as Eric Blair that he wished to be buried. So it is Eric Blair I would like others to remember, as I remember him.

In these recollections I have had the help of my sister Guinever : talking things over, one memory has led to another. Additionally, some useful information came to light in the Autumn of 1969 when we sold our last remaining house at Shiplake. It had been let for many years, with a large garden shed retained for storage, full of *bric-à-brac* and family papers. Among these oddments was a box put away in the 1920s, with letters from and about Eric, and my brother Prosper's diary for 1920. Prosper is now dead, but his *Schoolboy's Diary* gives the record of our many meetings with Eric in that year. There is Guiny's birthday book, given her for Christmas 1921, with the signature Eric Blair on his birthday, 25 June; and some photographs, with other items of contemporary evidence for events of over fifty years ago.

Sometimes biographers are criticised for falling to the level of 'Keats' Laundry-list', but even a laundry-list may give useful sidelights. If, for the week ending 19 May, the Great Man sent fifty-four pocket-handkerchiefs to the wash, but not a single pair of socks, it might provoke a never-ending controversy as to whether he spent that week in bed with a shocking snuffling cold or whether – as advocated by the rival faction – it could be read as proof that he had experimented with barefoot Morris dancing.

So I ask pardon for indulging in everyday trifles. Once I, with Eric's sister Avril and my sister Guiny, have passed that bourne from whence no traveller returns, there will no longer be any chance of a first-hand record of his home life in the early years.

It will be necessary for Buddicoms to be included in some detail, because so much of Eric's life was spent with us in the school holidays that he was almost part of our family. Our background and his were so closely interwoven that to understand what sort of boy the young Eric was at home, one must also know what kind of children the young Buddicoms were. Why did he choose us so steadfastly to be his closest – almost his only – friends? The answer is his own secret.

The world we all lived in was vastly different in its customs, its manners, and its values, from the world as it is today.

J.B.

Sussex, 1974

I

Buddicom Background

THERE WERE THREE Buddicom children, of whom I was the eldest: Jacintha Laura May, born 10 May 1901 at Plymouth, where my father Robert Arthur Buddicom (RAB) was curator of the Museum. He enjoyed this work very much, but, partly because the authorities would not allow him as free a hand as he required, and partly because my mother did not like to be so far from her own family then living in London, he resigned and left Plymouth when I was six weeks old.

My mother always thought of herself as Australian. Like her own mother she was born in Sydney. Her great-grandfather, a Gedye from St Neots, Cornwall, had been ordered a long sea-voyage for his health. His cousin Henry Dangar had gone out to Australia in 1821 as a prosaic surveyor – it would have been far more romantic if we could have claimed kinship with one of the early convict-settlers – and the Gedye cousin calling on him was so delighted with the country that he transferred there with all his family. His son, Charles Townsend Gedye, joined with other cousins in the Sydney firm now known as Dangar, Gedye & Malloch, still flourishing.

But C T Gedye had no son to succeed him in the business, and eventually he retired to England to live in London at 17 Craven Hill Gardens, where an elaborate music-room was the first essential. Greenie (as my mother always called him) was Mad About Music. His three daughters had to learn to play the piano – and to play it *well*, his granddaughters, my mother, and her sister, sang. Both had pretty, though not concert-class voices, and my mother in addition played the violin. My mother, who adored Greenie and told us many tales about him, said he frequently gave musical parties at which minor celebrities of the day performed.

On one occasion, after the dinner was eaten, the company duly assembled in the music-room seemed to be spending far too much time in inconsequential chatter. So Greenie, anxious for the musical feast to begin, leant over the reigning Songstress and whispered in her ear, '*Tempus fugit.*' She, misinterpreting this as a heavy hint that welcome had been outstayed, immediately got up and said 'Goodbye!' And the rest of the guests followed suit.

My mother's father, Reginald Finlay, was Scottish. Visiting Australia, he met and married my grandmother, Greenie's eldest daughter, there. The Finlays were a rather highbrow, cosmopolitan lot: his father was Professor of Languages at Glasgow University, and I was told could speak fifteen of them. My mother and her sister (Auntie Mimi) were educated rather extensively in France, Germany, and Switzerland, like their Finlay Aunts, and Auntie Mimi had a year in Italy as well to learn singing. Greenie's wife, my great-grandmother who died young, could paint. We have some attractive Australian scenes of the 1850's which she exhibited, and was praised for, at the Paris Salon. I don't know why she sent them there and not to the Royal Academy.

My father won a classical scholarship to Charterhouse, but moved to Uppingham which had a better reputation for science, which he preferred. He wanted to be an engineer, but was advised by his great-uncle William Barber Buddicom that the day of engineering had passed. This seems odd advice from the man who built the French Railways, and whose locomotive, *Le Buddicom*, the pride of the Mulhouse Museum, can work as well today as when it was made in 1844. However, my father went to Oxford instead with a Biological Scholarship, and after he had acquired an honours degree in the School of Physiology and the Naples Chair, prowled round Europe and North Africa on the track of antiquities, for which he had a catholic passion. His own family lived in Shropshire, where his father was a country squire of modest calibre, and his grandfather a parson who retired early to devote more time to collecting books in any interstices left by his other hobby of matrimony. He was married four times, and used to chant:

If I survive
I'll make it five

– but the fourth wife, much younger than himself and very pretty, outlived him.

My father became a Fellow of the Museums Association and the Geological Society. Geology was a subject in which my mother was also interested at that time, and it was at some function of the Society that they first met.

A year or two after he left the Plymouth Museum, having meantime done a bit of lecturing in London, my father, RAB, decided to go in for market-gardening. The Bolney Estate at Shiplake-on-Thames was up for sale: so, together with my mother's brother, Roy Finlay, and a friend, Frederick William Norsworthy, he bought a tract of this land reaching from the railway line up to the main Reading-Henley road. The lower portion being convenient for transport was laid out as market-gardens, with an expanse of glasshouses, boilerhouses, etc. The middle section consisted mainly of orchards for my uncle. And, on the upper part, houses were built to their own designs: three

3

as close as possible to the common edge of their respective boundaries, for neighbourliness.

The largest, Quarry House, for my parents, turned out larger than intended: when it was half-way up, RAB dashed off to Germany to hear some special performance of the Rhinegold, for which he had a peculiar partiality, and on his return found that an unexpected third story had been superimposed. The men explained that they had a few bricks left over and thought they might as well make use of them. Those were the days. It was called Quarry House because part of its grounds had been a gravel-pit.

My uncle had started some foundations almost touching Quarry House, but RAB said they were *too* close: so Uncle Dudie (as we called him) relinquished them and restarted his house just a very few yards further to the east, christening it Trevone after a place in Cornwall where RAB had helped to excavate a prehistoric burial-ground. Instead of abandoning the 'too-close' foundations, RAB went on with them to complete the four-bedroomed Quaint Cottage which he rented to the Finlay parents. This was a fairly ordinary, quite pleasant little place with a mansard roof: Trevone was much *quainter*. It had a Griffin over the porch, and Uncle Dudie designed it on the principle that the smell of food went upwards, so the kitchen and dining-room were on the first floor and the draw-ing-room and three best bedrooms downstairs – or they were supposed to be. But when the roof was on, and everything else completed, it was discovered that there *were* no stairs: they had been accidentally left out. So a fearfully narrow staircase was hastily stuck in, in the only place possible for it, like a ship's companionway.

Away from these three houses, close to the road, was a wooden bungalow with very small rooms and a very large verandah, which started tiny as an abode for Freddie Nors-worthy (known as NORS) and named The Shanty, but which was later enlarged and retitled Rambler Cottage.

4

Except for Nors, who persevered with his part of the project until he joined the army for the 1914-18 War, this horticultural adventure did not occupy the attention of the others for very long. The first time they offered their produce at Covent Garden, being strangers in those parts, they had all arrayed themselves in their conventional city suits – top hats, morning coats, striped trousers and all – and were roared at by the Cockney porters: 'Look out! 'Ere come our college chums!'

RAB went back to lecturing, at London Hospital Medical College and Birkbeck College. Grannifather Finlay, with an ingrained habit of wider spaces, found no appeal in what he called 'being cramped' in a small cottage belonging to his son-in-law, so he took a long lease of an enormous house with a river frontage at nearby Henley, early in 1906. But at the Easter of that year, while staying in London, he unexpectedly died. Uncle Dudie, left with this white elephant on his hands and never at a loss for an idea, found the then quite novel solution of turning it into a country club, I think the first of that particular type. So it became Phyllis Court Club, as which it still continues. The glasshouses were taken over by a family named Harding, 'Old Mr Harding' being eventually succeeded by his son. His daughter Milly Harding pioneered in a different way: she became the first feminine Bank Manager in England.

I remember Grannifather Finlay quite well, though I was not yet five when he died. He taught me the *alphabet*, a landmark of tremendous importance. Just before his death he had bought for us children Teddy Bears dressed as policemen, to be our Easter presents. But we were never allowed to touch them. They were kept on top of a high bookcase in the nursery, to be looked at only. On the day my sister Guinever was born, Sunday, 3 February 1907, our mother and the nurse being otherwise occupied, RAB was in charge of Prosper and me. So to keep us quiet, *we were allowed to play with Grannifather's bears*. Below the mantelpiece of the nursery fireplace was an Edwardian cast-iron panel above the grate, with a relief of blackbirds looking for worms. This was painted black, but on that red-letter day when Guiny was born, RAB picked out their beaks in yellow, and their legs and the worm in pink.

The Quarry House nursery was a good-sized, interestingly-shaped room on the first floor, with a glass door to the balcony. It was painted dark green up to table height, which was useful for drawing on with white chalk because it showed up well and would wash off. Above was a frieze of Noah's Ark and all the animals, and above that again, cream walls with silhouettes of every member of the family. RAB made these by having a candle held in front of the person to be drawn, tracing round the shadow thrown on the wall, and painting it black with a small white lozenge left at the lower edge for the sitter's initials. All this original decoration was scrapped when we grew up and the room was used as our mother's study: but that was the way it was when the young Blairs first played in it with us.

The advent of Guiny is not my earliest memory: that was my second birthday party, which took place at 17 Craven Hill Gardens on 10 May 1903. I can see now the table set out with a fine white cloth – from the height of being *below* the top of the table, which I was not tall enough to reach without being held up. And I can recall still the ecstatic delirium of realising that these *wonderful* presents, this *glorious* cake with pink sugar icing and *two lighted candles*, were *all* for *me*. It was the first time I realised I had an identity.

About 1910 Number Seventeen was given up as being too big, and Gran Finlay moved to a house in Bournemouth acclaimed 'more manageable', with the idea that her sisters should live there too. But one, Auntie Floss, widowed a few years earlier, died: and the other, Toddie, suddenly married and went to live with her husband Edward Lovell-Clare in Cheyne Walk by the Chelsea Embankment.

A sidelight on the changing face of Britain: Burwood Glen,

St Stephen's Road, was a house with drawing-room, dining-room, very big hall used as a sitting-room, small library, and large music-room (in the Gedye tradition) to contain a concert grand – there was an upright piano as well, in the drawing-room. Upstairs were seven bedrooms, two with dressing-rooms, as well as maids' rooms and domestic offices on both floors, porches, and conservatories. The gardens stretched right to St Stephen's Church, with a wild sloping part full of fir trees, rose-garden, tennis and croquet courts on the lower level, and a stable block housing Gran's car with chauffeur's quarters over. It was not considered at all too extensive for a widow in her early fifties (even without the companionship of her sisters), who with an income enabling her to live in reasonable comfort, was by no means *rich*: I don't suppose she had more than £1,000 a year. Nowadays she would be more likely to retire to a two-roomed, fourthfloor flat, at a rent six times the rent of Burwood Glen.

After Gran died in 1933, none of the family wanted to live in Bournemouth, so the house was relinquished. The authorities constructed a new thoroughfare, Braidley Road, beside the old Church, where Gran's tennis and croquet courts used to be, and several houses were built beside it in place of the rose-garden. The stable block became yet another house, and later on Burwood Glen itself, conveniently opposite the Town Hall, was used for Local Government offices. (I am told it is now pulled down, and something else put up instead.)

The Blairs had an uncle living in Bournemouth, with whom they sometimes stayed in the summer holidays, as we did with our grandmother. But I can only once remember these visits coinciding and Eric having tea at Burwood. The uncle never proffered a return-invitation – to me, at any rate. I think Prosper went for one or two walks with Eric.

Robert Prosper Gedye, the middle child of our family, was born at Quarry House on 15 July 1904. We usually lived at

Quarry House, but in 1914 my mother built a new and attractive little thatched cottage in a big hilly field to the north-west. Uncle Dudie had built himself a thatched cottage on his own north-west boundary line a few years earlier, and my mother thought it would be nice to have one too: there was a very good thatcher in Henley. We were in the thatched cottage for a couple of summers, going back to Quarry House for the winter: and, after it was enlarged, we occasionally spent the summer at The Shanty. Our mother depended for extra income on letting the houses furnished, and Quarry House (with three sitting-rooms and seven bedrooms much the largest and grandest) got the biggest rent. In those days 'The River' was just as popular as 'The Seaside' for summer sojourns, and houses at Shiplake were in great demand – there were so few of them. Some people had house-boats, moored along the river bank; mostly rich people like the Vanderbilts.

The houseboats looked enchanting at night, decorated with fairy lights and Japanese lanterns. We were taken once to see them, and for a moonlight picnic, in the punt. Most people had punts, if they did not have skiffs or dinghies: skiffs were more sporting, but punts were much more comfortable. It was chiefly the grown-ups who had the picnic, and Prosper and Guiny slept most of the time. But I stayed awake to this dream world of flickering lanterns, and lovely ladies with lots of frills, and men with the scent of cigars, and music: singing and laughter floating across the reflections in the water.

We ourselves usually went to the seaside for holidays: when Gran lived there, to Bournemouth, before that to a different place every year. In August 1908 we had a protracted tour of Devon and Cornwall, revisiting my birthplace at Plymouth, but mainly staying in a rented house at Newquay by the estuary. It was exciting and fearful to watch the tide swooshing up to cover the smooth sand that was the bed of the tidal river. 'Supposing we hadn't *known* – and had gone to play sand-castles there –!'

There are photos of this tour: one taken by RAB at Newquay of the three children — Guiny a roly-poly eighteen months, and Prosper having almost caught up with me in size — with our mother and the nurse, Nurse Allie, whom I loved very dearly. She was quite young, with dark hair and very rosy cheeks, and she was always kind: the previous, rapidly-evicted, nurse had *not* been kind. Nurse Allie had a wealth of happy games, and songs, and stories, and she taught me how to make pink paper boxes: I can make them still. She left us to train as a hospital nurse 'to better herself', when we were old enough for a French governess. A few years later she wrote to our mother that she was going to be married, and our mother sent a wedding present: but, quite uncharacteristically of Nurse Allie, received no acknowledgment. The next we saw of her she was in the headlines. She was Alice Burnham, the second Bride in the Bath. It was a proper satisfaction when George Joseph Smith was hanged by the neck until he was dead. Capital punishment is a great deterrent to murder: at least the same murderer does not get the chance to murder again.

In the first years at Shiplake, we were surrounded by fields, and from Quarry House windows we could see the lights of the trains at night along the railway line. But later on the the fields on our south boundary were divided up into building plots, each of about an acre, on which fair-sized houses were built to front the adjoining lane. The most westerly of these houses was Rose Lawn. And the lane became Station Road. And the trains could not be seen any more, nor even heard so well.

RAB lived more and more in London, spending increasingly infrequent weekends with us at Shiplake. On rare occasions, I had the *TREAT OF A DAY IN TOWN* with him, being seen off at Shiplake Station, travelling grandly by myself, and being met by RAB at Paddington. Matinees were usually included in these programmes: one was *A White Man*, another was *Tom Jones*. The best of all these treats was *a visit to the British Museum*, where RAB had promised we should be meeting

'A Great Egyptologist'. Egyptian images were already very familiar to me: RAB had a nice little collection of them in a glass-fronted cupboard over the drawing-room mantelpiece. But I had never heard the word *Egyptologist* before. So when we forgathered with RAB's old friend Dr Wallis Budge, accompanied unexpectedly by Lord Carnarvon, I thought they were two of the Egyptian Gods. (*Naturally* they would be wearing ordinary clothes – they would not arrive to meet people at the British Museum in full panoply of Hawks' Heads and What Have You – the *King* would not wear his crown just to go out to tea, would he?) For a very long time I cherished this happy illusion, since it never occurred to me to discuss it with RAB till he gave me his own *Egyptian Gods* in 1915, as a parting present, and I was informed of the true identity of these personages.

In February 1915 RAB insisted on swapping his land at Shiplake for a plot at Turramurra left to my mother by her Gedye grandfather, and went off to Australia for ever.

And to those liberated women who bleat permissively that they *prefer* to be unmarried mothers, that it is so *nice* for their children to be disburdened of a father cluttering up the place, I would give assurance that, from the child's point of view, it most emphatically is *not*. If a father turns out badly, if he is cruel and ill-natured, by all means get rid of him. If he repudiates his responsibilities, it is a tragedy. But it is unwarrantable for a woman, in sheer inconsiderate conceit, deliberately to refuse to get married, and deliberately deprive her child of half a normal family life.

2

The Blairs

WE WERE PLAYING French cricket in the roughish field-part of the Thatched Cottage garden, by the clump of elm trees : Prosper, Guiny and I, with Nors; as near as possible to the other side of the wire fence separating us from the farmer's adjoining meadow, a boy rather bigger than Prosper was standing on his head.

This was a feat we had not observed before, and we found it intriguing. So, after a while, Nors asked him :

'Why are you standing on your head ?'

To which he replied :

'You are noticed more if you stand on your head than if you are right way up.'

So we did what was obviously hoped for, and asked him to come over and play with us. He said his name was Eric Blair and that he lived at Rose Lawn in the Station Road. And from that sunny, summer afternoon, we were all very close friends indeed.

The time of this first meeting can be tracked down fairly well, thanks to the box of papers unearthed at Shiplake in

1969. There is a letter from RAB, written on paper with the printed heading *The London Hospital Medical College, University of London*, dated 3 June 1914, and addressed to me at 'The Hawthorns, Nettlebed'. This not only proves where RAB was working at the time, but also pinpoints the year the Thatched Cottage was built: we stayed in rooms at Nettlebed because it was not quite ready for occupation, and Quarry House was let. There are also photographs taken at our Great-Aunt Maria Jenkins' home in Shropshire, one of which is annotated by our mother, 'Charlton Hill, Wroxeter, Tuesday September 8th 1914'. So the meeting with Eric must have taken place just before, or just after, that visit. It was certainly very hot and sunny, and in the holidays, as both boys were at their prep schools in term time: Prosper at The Old Ride, Branksome Park, and Eric at St Cyprian's, Eastbourne. We were back at Quarry House for the winter: there is a Buddicom Christmas Card printed with the Quarry House address, and with Allied Flags as decoration.

There were three young Blairs: two girls with a boy in the middle, like the young Buddicoms, but the Blairs were spaced wider apart – five years between each instead of three, as we were. Marjorie, born 21 April 1898, would have been sixteen in 1914. She never played with us, and we thought her 'quite grown-up'. We did not often see her in those days, but she and I were both confirmed – according to my confirmation-class card – on Sunday 21 February 1915 in Henley. I was rather young for confirmation at thirteen, she at sixteen a more usual age.

Marjorie and her mother seemed particularly fond of each other, with many common interests, so, except when separated by their war-work, they spent a lot of time together. As far as I can remember they looked rather alike, too. Mrs Blair had curly hair in those days. (Perhaps she put it up in paper curlers at night, like Gran, or had it marcel-waved in this pre-perm era?) The photo of an unsmiling lady with a short straight fringe, dated 1937 and put out of context in *The World of George Orwell*, does not much resemble the vivacious, spirited Mrs Blair I knew. But I never saw her in 1937, and of course people do change with time.

Avril, the baby of the family, was born on 6 April 1908, and was a year younger than Guiny, So the two little girls were of an age to be playmates.

Eric, born on 25 June 1903, was a year older than Prosper and two years younger than me – but fairly equivalent to us both. He was so much larger and cleverer than I was that the two-year difference was hardly noticeable: and, on the other hand, Prosper with RAB and Nors and Uncle Dudie around had perhaps had some better example of boyish pursuits in his home life than Eric, with only his mother and sisters till he was eight, and such an elderly father afterwards.

I am indebted to the chronology of the *Orwell Archive* for the dates of birth of the older Blairs, which are worth considering. Eric's mother Ida Mabel Blair, known and signed as Ida, was born in 1875, so was contemporary with our own parents: RAB born 7 November 1874 and our mother 25 July 1877. (Nors and Uncle Dudie were both born in 1881, and in between came our two aunts – our father's sister Lilian, born 8 December 1878, and our mother's sister Mimi born 15 August 1879.)

But Eric's father Richard Walmesley Blair (called Dick) was born on 7 January 1857, so belonged to the previous generation: Gran Finlay was only two when he was born, and *older* than her sister. He certainly seemed to us children to be very ancient and not sympathetic. He was not *unkind* – he never beat Eric (though RAB once gave Prosper a well-deserved spanking) but he did not understand, nor, I think, much care for children – after all, he hardly saw his own till he was fifty. He always seemed to expect us all to keep rather out of his way, which we were reciprocatively glad to do. This was not difficult as he was usually at the Golf Club, where he worked as secretary as well as playing a good deal of golf himself, before and after his army service in the war. Very sportingly, he joined up. It seems a bit extraordinary that they took him, since at sixty he was reputed to be the oldest subaltern in the British Army, but he even went to France. His late marriage and fatherhood carried on his family's tradition. The young Blairs never knew their paternal grandfather, the Reverend Thomas Richard Arthur Blair, who died aged sixty-five in 1867 – over thirty years before his son Richard had his first child at the age of forty-one. The timespan of these male Blairs seems fantastic : Eric's grandfather was born in 1802 – a hundred and one years before Eric. Our Grandpapa Buddicom was born in 1840, and our great-grandfather Gedye in 1833. So Eric's grandfather was old enough to have been our *grandparents*' grandfather! Eric disapproved of exclamation marks, but this feat deserves several.

Both Eric's parents belonged to large Victorian families, so the young Blairs had quite a number of uncles and aunts. Some, Eric told us, had a family business in Burma, but others lived in England. Strangely, we never saw any of them. If they ever came to Shiplake or Henley to visit the Blairs, we were never invited to meet them : though Eric talked about his mother's sisters, the Limouzins, whom he irreverently nicknamed 'The Lemonskins', or 'The Automobiles'. I asked why not just 'Motorcars', but he explained that Automobiles, like the Limouzins themselves, were French. There was an Aunt Ivy Limouzin and an Aunt Nellie, as I remember. One or two of these aunts and their friends were Militant Suffragettes. Mrs Blair was in sympathy, but not so active. *Some* of this contingent, Eric said, went to prison and on hunger-strike as well as more moderately chaining themselves to railings. My mother thought that women ought to have the vote, but she disapproved of

violence. We were all very shocked indeed when the Suffragettes set fire to Wargrave Church, just across the river.

Some of these relations of Eric's were Fabians, and he went
with one of his aunts to visit E Nesbit. As the Arden and Psam-
mead books were among my favourites, I was rather envious
of this privilege. That early Fabian influence may have been
what first set his thoughts on pure Socialism : though I have
not seen it recorded in any writings about him that a Fabian
atmosphere was the natural habitat of some of his relatives.
It is surprising that a fact of such apparently relevant importance should have been omitted. I'm not sure whether he
actually met H G Wells too, besides E Nesbit, in those early
days, though he certainly did later. I *do* remember his coming
home from either the same, or possibly another, visit to the
Fabian Aunt and grizzling interminably that he had *just
missed H G Wells* – so disappointed that I wondered if he
would ever smile again. But of course he soon recovered : Eric
was almost invariably a cheerful boy.

It does seem a little peculiar that we never met any of these
relations. But I don't think that the parent Blairs, at any rate
in those days, had much time for young visitors. The Blair
parents were always very formal : we always called them 'Mr
Blair' and 'Mrs Blair', never a courtesy 'Uncle Dick' or 'Auntie
Ida', or nicknames, as we did with so many of our own elders'
friends : Aunt Nettie for Miss Auden, The Goon for Captain
Paget, or even just Dom and Nina for the equally 'ancient'
Dalys.

Eric, often accompanied by Avril, played in our garden
practically every day : but we comparatively seldom played in
theirs. This may have been chiefly because ours was bigger and
better for playing, with a lot of wild part : the former gravel-
pit was now a steep, grass-covered bank down from the road,
and there was a mini-forest of fir trees. Each New Year we had
a ceremony when our Christmas Tree was planted in the

gravel-pit : they grew up very fast and tall – they are simply terrific now – and were augmented by a few extra ones. There was, too, the field between the Thatched Cottage and the other houses, also steep and grassy, down which we rode dangerously on our bicycles. We often played bicycle-polo on the croquet-lawn, with croquet-balls and mallets, as a change from the more commonplace game on foot : and *robber* was preferred to *straight* croquet. The Blairs' was a much more conventional laid-out garden, with a potent if unwritten notice : *Keep off the flowerbeds.*

Rose Lawn had a long garden, with the front entrance to the south on Station Road. At the far north end of the ground was a rather overgrown hedge which formed a common boundary with the Quarry House kitchen-garden. In the school holidays before Eric sat for his scholarships he had extra correspondence-coaching from one of the St Cyprian's masters. Often, when we were all playing in the Quarry House garden, Mr Blair would come down and call over this hedge to Eric, reminding him to be sure to get his homework done in time to catch the post. And if he had left it a bit late, he had to return home at once – even if it were in the middle of a game. Children could crawl through the thinnest part of the hedge, but the sedate Mr Blair had to stay in his own domain or walk round by the road.

Avril sometimes played with a little girl called Mimi Dakin, whose father was a doctor in Henley – but not our doctor, who belonged to the 'rival firm' : we did not know the Dakins ourselves. Little Mimi's much older brother Humphrey married Marjorie in 1920, and he has been mentioned as the leader aged fifteen of a 'gang' of his own contemporaries, with whom Eric was very occasionally allowed to 'tag along' at the age of seven, when the Blairs were living in Henley. We did not know Eric at the age of seven, but by the time he was eleven, when we did, there was no sign of association with anyone else at all. Although members of a family may string along in a linked chain from the eldest to the youngest, among boys not related there is a vast difference between a *big boy* of fifteen and a *little kid* of seven: thus, much involvement between Eric and the 'gang' sounds hardly practicable. At any rate, in all the years we knew Eric, we cannot recall his being accompanied by any friends, or any contemporaries with him in the Blair home, or his having schoolfriends to stay and exchange visits as Prosper often did in the holidays. Of course, Shiplake was a very small place at that time, mostly inhabited by fairly elderly people. We had very few contemporaries and these were not permanent residents, nor did their parents seem to congregate with the Blair parents.

There were the exotic Ardizzones who often came to stay with their grandmother, fierce and forbidding Mrs Irving. I can remember a Christmas party at her big house on the hill – but this might have been in the days before we knew the Blairs – and many later summer parties at the smaller (but we thought more exciting) house beside the river to which she moved. The Ardizzones were a large family: two girls close in age to me, both nice and both pretty, but Tetta was particularly pretty and Betty was particularly nice: two small brothers younger than Guiny, Michael and David, who always did everything together though they were not twins: and Ted, the eldest of the family, very dignified and portly, who drew far better than anybody else when we played Heads-bodies-and-legs, long, long before he was Edward Ardizzone with pictures not only in the Tate and many books to his credit. Occasionally a small and sweet girl cousin, the little orphaned Mary about the same age as David, stayed with their grandmother too: *she* grew up to be Christianna Brand. With Ted and Mary I still have contact, but so many of the others alas are not now alive. They were such a happy and interesting family, and we welcomed their visits to Mrs Irving, whose son Alec was a great friend of Nors.

There were the even more exotic Carrerases, an even larger

family, because, whereas the Ardizzones only had one cousin, the Carrerases seemed to have dozens: a fiesta of birds of paradise on flying visits, Spanish and beautiful, with beautiful Spanish names: Carmencita, Conchita-Chiquita-Rosita, Maria-Teressa, Pilar – I am not sure if they were really *all* their names. There is a suspicion that because I admired their unfamiliar charm so very extravagantly, they kindly provided themselves with a few extra besides those they received at their christenings. They were mostly girls or grown-ups (perhaps older brothers were at the War) but there was a very much younger boy, little Jimmy as often as not called Hymie (Jaime, I suppose). Once one of the older girls tied her white hair-ribbon in a band round his head, and he was very much affronted, saying boys didn't wear hair-ribbons. But one of the exquisite sisters or cousins picked up a chicken feather and stuck it in the bandeau, telling him he was now an Indian Brave – at which he was quite consoled. I haven't seen any of that family for more than fifty years. Perhaps he is now Sir James Carreras of the Horror Films?

They had a most gorgeous dog, a magnificent St Bernard, exuberant and friendly. Once when we went to lunch with them he gently put his paws on RAB's shoulders to greet him, and knocked him over backwards. Another time they brought him to tea with us, in the garden, and I patted him. This displeased my Blue Persian Quillie, equally affectionate and a very possessive little cat. She arched her back and spat at him, so that he turned tail, very much abashed, and I dared not pat him again.

The Carrerases and Mrs Irving were great party-givers: and when not involved with the War, Uncle Dudie and our mother had frequent visitors. But the only real party I can recall the Blairs giving was a Christmas party at Rose Lawn, when Marjorie and her friend, the other Marjorie/Margery Dakin sang. This must have been the Christmas of 1914 or 1915: and nearly everyone there seemed to be grown-up.

Although Eric may not have known other children at Ship-lake on account of their scarcity, before and after Rose Lawn the Blairs lived in Henley where there must have been plenty of children he could have got to know *if* he had wanted to. The way he manoeuvred acquaintance with us proved him quite capable of ingeniously making friends with a family he liked the look of: you *are* noticed more if you ostentatiously stand on your head – incidentally not the behaviour of such a cringing, inhibited little misery as he is posthumously alleged to have been.

But having found and, apparently, been well pleased with us, I do not think he needed any other friends beyond the schoolfriend he occasionally and appreciatively referred to as 'CC': presumably Cyril Connolly, but the full name was never mentioned and I never met him. Eric was a naturally reserved and rather self-contained boy: and we three Buddi-coms, in our different ways, between us shared his interests and gave him all the companionship he wished for outside his family.*

The Blairs, though certainly not demonstrative, were never-theless a united family, and their home seemed to us to be a happy one. I do not think Eric was *fond* of his father, although he respected and obeyed him, but without any doubt he was genuinely fond of his mother and sisters, especially Avril. Eric and Avril were in those days rather similar in appearance, rather plump, round-faced children – 'moon-faced' Eric des-cribed himself. He was always very kind to Avril when they played with us, and equally kind to Guiny. Avril and Guiny

*His sister Avril wrote to me on 14 March 1973: 'I think Eric had all the friends, and the sort of friends, that he wanted. In any case, he was essen-tially an aloof, undemonstrative person, which doesn't necessarily mean to say that he had a blighted childhood and developed a 'death wish' as so many biographers seem to think. I do hope that your publication will clear this issue.' And in a later letter, after I had sent her a further draft of this memoir to inspect for accuracy, on 11 April she says: 'You seem to be get-ting on well and making a very fair assessment of Eric's boyhood.'

19

were 'the little ones', consequently simply by reason of their lesser age and strength, the parents did not always consider it suitable for them to join in expeditions more appropriate for the older children. I remember Avril kicking at the gate, mourning dolefully, 'Oh! I do wish I was go-wing!', and Eric, after admonishing her good-humouredly: 'Oh! Dry up, Avril!', returning to the house to get permission for her to come after all.

Through all the years it would seem that his feeling for his family remained constant: it was his sister Avril he asked to come and keep house for him after his wife Eileen died, and it was for his father he named his adopted son Richard. (For Richard Rees too, perhaps: but he did not *avoid* the name because it was his father's.) He did not like his own name Eric, as it reminded him of the Victorian boys' school story *Eric or Little by Little*, a book he deplored. Again, through all the years he kept in close touch with his family: in Burma, seeing his Burma-based relations; in Paris his Aunt Nellie; and back in England often staying at Southwold or with Marjorie.

The fact that he criticised his parents was to be expected of someone with his temperament: he fancied himself as a critic from his earliest youth. Few books were read without the most detailed and meticulous criticism – '*stern critic*' Cyril Connolly apostrophises him at the age of thirteen, requesting a sample of his work. Behaviour of high or low came in for equal review and comment, but there was never any malice in it. Eric was not a malicious or quarrelsome boy: he had, I think, a quite unusually calm and philosophical temperament, and a shrewd sense of humour. Prosper and I quarrelled from time to time. We had our faults: I was selfish and he was greedy, so our disputes were usually on the well-worn theme of his trying to grab something of mine, and my hanging on to it as my private personal possession. But if we argued when Eric was there, he generally kept the peace. Guiny, little 'Golden Guinea', good as gold, never in her life ever quarrelled with anyone. As the third in our family, she was probably better managed with more practice. And she had the great advantage of being a Sunday Baby :

> The child that is born on the Sabbath day
> Is blithe and bonny, and good and gay.

The only time I can remember quarrelling with Eric myself was when he and Prosper killed a beautiful hedgehog – an animal for which I have particular affection – and baked it in clay as they had heard the gipsies did. I would not speak to them for a week. Our cook was not best pleased when she found this already sepulchred corpse in the oven : but when, a few days later, they set up an amateur whisky-still on top of the kitchen stove while she was having her afternoon rest, and the whole contraption blew up, she gave notice.

This was not their only explosion. They were both very keen on what they called *chemical experiments*, and another time they lit a bonfire in the garden and put in some home-made gunpowder. No expected conflagration occurred, so Eric gave the fire a good poke to see why it hadn't gone off. Where-upon it immediately did. Luckily they were not such expert manufacturers of gunpowder as they imagined themselves to be, so Eric lost no more than a few eyebrows. But both boys had very black clothes and hands and faces, and the Elders were justly annoyed.

Although his 1914 headstand was our first conscious meet-ing with Eric, he and Prosper must have been together in the baby class at the Anglican Convent School in Henley. Prosper and I went there for a brief time one spring and summer, when he was four and I was seven. The nuns were not very enthusias-tic about little boys, and would only admit them young enough for the baby class. Prosper, unfortunately, was at that period rather a belligerent child : and when rebuked by the nuns for fighting with another little boy (quite possibly Eric himself, aged five?) he called them *damn devils*. This finished off any former tolerance completely, and they declared that after the end of term they would have no little boys at all. I was most frightfully upset: I *loved* school. Besides the fun of other children to play with, there was the interesting *work*. Instead of marks we had pretty cards called 'exemptions' (French pronunciation) all in different colours for differing degrees of proficiency, which were collected by each child in its own special box to fit and counted at the end of term. The child with best exemptions got a prize, in each class at the end-of-term summer party, where we all sat on the grass under the trees in the big garden, and went up for our prizes one by one. In the younger children's classes everyone was given a bar of chocolate, whether they had won a prize or not.

My mother decreed that if the nuns *would not* have Prosper, they *should not* have me: and that we must do lessons at home with a governess until he was old enough to go to prep school. I thought lessons with a governess very dull compared with glorious *school* and lots of other little girls. I don't know whether, having tactfully got rid of the provocative Prosper, the nuns relented and kept Eric on.

Avril cannot possibly have been there when we were: she was then only a year old. Nor, I suppose, would she have been there with Eric, as he went to St Cyprian's when he was eight and she still only three. But Eric and Marjorie were doubtless pupils together, though I can't remember anything about her when I was there. Of course she would have been senior, in a higher class.

I don't recollect, either, the name Nutshell as a house of the Blairs at Henley: this would have been before we knew them at Rose Lawn. But I well remember Eric showing me a Henley house called Ermadale in Vicarage Road. He said they once lived in it, and that it was named after ERic and MArjorie.

Was this earlier than Nutshell, and Avril not yet born when it was named, perhaps? Eric seemed very fond of Ermadale: on several occasions later, when we went to or from the station and St Marks Road, Eric would choose to go the slightly longer way round, so as to pass Ermadale and touch the name on the gatepost. It seems to have disappeared completely now. A lot of the houses in Vicarage Road have been renamed or rebuilt.

I don't remember exactly when the Blairs went to live in St Marks Road, but it was certainly *after* Eric's scholarship-homework had been finished with.

Their removal from the fair-sized house, in nearly an acre of ground, to the semi-detached villa with a pocket-handker-chief front garden, did not occur because, as the Mystiquites would have it, the expense of Eric's Eton education – as a King's Scholar! – forced his parents to strict economy in every sphere. Although the change of home and change of school were roughly contemporary, it must be remembered – as usual – that there was a war on.

With the prospect of Mr Blair in the Army, Mrs Blair with war-work in London, Marjorie in the Women's Services of the time, the two younger children at boarding-school, and gardeners unobtainable, Rose Lawn became 'a beastly nuisance' impossible to look after: whereas the more modest 36 St Marks Road was conveniently compact and needed little attention.

3

Popular Pastimes

It may surprise some young people today, if they have not yet thought about it, to visualise the world in which we, in the first quarter of the century, lived. Television had not been invented, nor even radio: there were no coffee-bars, youth clubs, discotheques, teenage dance-halls, or other organisations providing us with built-in entertainment. Our entertainment was dependent on ourselves, though there was an occasional visit to the cinema, commonly called *The Pictures* – because that is what they were: we had no sound in those days, of course, just an appropriate piano accompaniment.

Guiny reminds me of an occasion when old Mr Blair was asked by Avril for a halfpenny. Though never begrudging small sums beyond regular pocket money, he was the sort of man who always required chapter and verse. So he enquired what she wanted it for, and she said, 'To go to the pictures'. Rather surprised, for he was seldom very conversant with his children's pursuits, he exclaimed, 'But surely you can't get into the cinema for a *halfpenny*?' To which the honest Avril answered, 'No, it's a penny – but I've got one halfpenny already.'

Things were much cheaper in those days. The front rows of seats were only a penny for children at the afternoon performance, and for threepence you could have a most luxurious time: a penny for the return fare Shiplake-to-Henley by train, a penny for the pictures themselves, and a penny for a vast choice of refreshment, especially if pooled between four or five.

A penny would buy twelve caramels each wrapped in separate paper, or ten bullseyes which weren't, so that, although they lasted longer, they were inclined to stick together inseparably, so making fair shares difficult to divide. A penny would buy two small bars of chocolate or one large one, each in five sections called *Fry's Five Boys*. It would buy two ha'penny buns, each the size of one costing 3p or 4p nowadays, or four farthing buns which had a larger expanse of tasty outside and sugar in proportion. It would buy a bottle of fizzy lemonade or raspberryade with an ingenious glass marble for a stopper instead of a cork – screw-tops hadn't been invented then, either.

For a penny, too, one could obtain large quantities of licorice allsorts (which still seem extant, though at a very different price) – tough black leathery things with pink and white sugar stripes which none of us liked. But Eric very occasionally bought them. He said they tasted *so* beastly that they were almost fascinating, and he wanted to make sure they were still as beastly as he had thought. They always were, and he always had to finish them himself as nobody else would touch them. The first remembrance was quite enough for us, without any further corroboration. We all much preferred Conversation Peppermints, hard flat discs of sugar – round, with moral aphorisms printed on them, heart-shaped with sentimental ones.

In the very early days we did not even have gramophones of our own, nor did our parents possess cars, which were still not in common use – though Uncle Dudie, always up-to-the-minute, had both. His first car in the very early 1900s was, I think, about the earliest in Shiplake. Our Shropshire relatives, and all the country houses, and houses with stables, had horses and carriages. But most people in places like Shiplake and Henley, with only a few minutes' walk to a station, just hired cabs (and later, taxis) for local visiting and otherwise travelled by train. The railway service was very good in those days: plenty of excellent quick trains at reasonable fares, and a bookstall at every station. Again a different world from the world of today.

For transport independent of trains, we had bicycles as soon as we were old enough: at other times we walked. There was also *The Venture*, which plied between Henley and Reading, described in its advertisement of 12 November 1915 as 'A Powerful 22-seat Motor Char-a-Banc', which ran once a day on Tuesdays and Fridays and three times a day on Wednesdays and Saturdays. *The Venture* was very fine indeed, dark green embellished with its name in gigantic gold script: but its fare was of equal proportions. Fourpence each way, Shiplake to Henley, made us perforce infrequent patrons. But we admired it very much, and at first stood by the side of the road at the end of our drive to wave to it: until rebuked by the driver, who kept stopping the bus thinking we were would-be passengers, and failed to appreciate our kind intention of merely being polite. Eric did suggest that we could have a *code*, but this did not please the driver any better.

Not-too-long country walks were a popular pursuit. Prosper, Eric, and Guiny were all very keen on natural history, especially birds, about which they knew quite a lot. They had several good bird books, and were constantly identifying species and collecting birds' eggs – not prohibited then, but you must only take *one* egg from a nest and not disturb the parent birds. There were a great many interesting birds at Shiplake in those days. A red-backed shrike nested in the may trees, there were wrynecks and turtle-doves in summer; and green woodpeckers. A number of plovers always made their nests in the ploughed fields, and we had a colony of goldcrests in the garden, besides many different tits and finches. Every year the nightingales came back, as did the swifts and swallows, and the house-martins which nested in the eaves of the balcony beside our nursery at Quarry House: and one got almost tired of hearing the cuckoo.

My own ornithology was confined to the easily recognisable: the blackbirds, sparrows, and thrushes, up to an occasional water-wagtail, were about my mark: for the others on the list, I am indebted to Guiny – the other children were much more knowledgeable. My favourite of all was the robin, who flew in through the fanlight of the dining-room window and helped himself to the butter-pats on the breakfast table.

On very many occasions in the spring and summer, we went down to the river, fishing: we did not take our fishing tensely, in pouring rain with umbrellas and macintoshes, as so many devotees are wont to do. For us, it had to be fine weather. And our favourite place was by Shiplake Lock, one of the prettiest walks in the village. The far side of the lock, bordered by trees, was not popular: though the boys sometimes thought that the fish would *bite* better there in the shade, if the day was very sunny. But trees were an inconvenient hazard for the lines, which had quite enough hazard in the clear meadows. Once Guiny and Avril, admittedly rather young at the time, only about seven and eight, got their lines tangled together before they had even started to fish, and although they spent the whole afternoon trying to get the tangle disengaged, they had not done so by the time we had to go home for tea. They were obliged to carry the rods back, still closely intertwined: the boys were too busy to help them, and they were too proud to let me.

The site we liked best was one of the little sandy bays along the river bank of the gently sloping meadows on the way to Shiplake Court – a big country house then belonging to the Phillimores, which is now a school for boys. There you could *see* the fish through the clear, shallow water. I did not do much fishing myself, but I nearly always accompanied the party to this attractive spot. There was no fly-fishing, even for the boys, in those early days: they used bread pellets, made at home beforehand, which were annoyingly snapped up by the swarming shoals of minnows before anything larger and more interesting had a chance to get near. Occasionally they used worms, collected from the garden, or slug-like 'gentles' bought by Eric in Henley.

Out of doors, the games we mostly played were croquet, rounders, and French cricket – because there were not enough of us for anything else. Nearly all gardens had tennis-courts (which of recent years have made profitable extra building-sites for their owners) but when the men of the family were away at the War, ours was not kept marked for tennis which we children did not play till the War was over.

With plenty of ground, our family always kept chickens and a cow. Ducks were tried, but though called Indian Runners, they did not run – they flew, right away, never to be seen again. Probably they preferred the nearby river where they had plenty of company in the way of moorhens, dabchicks, and swans with seasonal cygnets. During the war, we also had a pig. He was called *Aw-pig* because he was so awful. There was an old man from a nearby farm to look after all this livestock, but Guiny, an outdoor girl, found it all very interesting and learnt to milk the cow and look after the fowls etc. At one time she had a pony called Rampumiam because he was rather rampant and she was the only person who could manage him. I did not care for all these species: I preferred cats in practice and mice in theory – that is to say, I thought them pretty little creatures but never wanted to keep mice as pets. Prosper and

Guiny kept rabbits and a ferret – not together – and Guiny had a tame jackdaw.

Avril says that the Blairs had quite a series of pets in the Shiplake days: Tojo, a wirehaired terrier, a black Aberdeen terrier (name forgotten), Marjorie's guineapigs – notably *Gussie* who produced a phenomenal number of offspring – and of course various cats.

We had constant cats, mostly Blue Persians. Mine was Quillie, and her husband, Mannie belonged to Guiny. They had a lot of kittens and went to cat-shows and won numerous prizes. After the first time she was sent to a cat-show in a basket with her kittens, in spite of the red First Prize Labels with which she returned, Quillie firmly avoided going again. Whenever the basket was brought out she was not to be found until after the show-party had safely started on their journey. So the kittens were accompanied by Mannie, who looked after them and washed them and was greatly admired. He was a very Gentil Parfit Cat: he always let Quillie and the kittens eat first at mealtimes, and never spat or scratched at anyone or anything. Quillie was the hunter.

But Prosper and I got diphtheria, and Mannie caught it from us and died. I had measles, too, and all the time I was ill, Quillie brought me what she considered a titbit every day – mice, or birds, or young rabbits, and once a weasel. At the end of the holidays, when my trunk was being packed for school, she always knew what it meant and walked round, and round, and round it, crying miserably. She was my special cat and I was her special person.

But one half-term when I came home she was not there. She had disappeared about a week previously, and no one had made much effort to discover what had become of her. I searched and searched but she was never found.

I think Eric was the only person who understood how desolating the loss of Quillie was to me. My mother took the atti-

29

tude that it was a pity about Quillie, but there were other cats, and why couldn't I be as philosophical as I had been about the untimely death of Mannie? Prosper and Guiny, with so many pets of so many kinds, were sorry, but held rather the same view. But Eric realised how precious one particular companion could be, and how different was Quillie's disappearance from the death of Mannie. Mannie I very, very much regretted : but it was at least a known and certain thing. With Quillie, it was *not knowing* that was so awful : not knowing, and when she had loved and trusted me so much, not being there. It never ceased to haunt me, and I did not have another cat for thirty years.

We had different dogs at different times. The last, a black and tan terrier called Bobby, was rather a favourite of Eric's, to whom we gave him when the Blairs went to Southwold. Bobby suffered from asthma, and we thought the sea air might do him good. But he died after quite a short time. I don't remember the Blairs' other animals, but I remember some cats. The last one, a big tabby, I think was taken over by their nice maid, May (a local farmer's daughter), when they let 36 St Marks Road.

When it was wet or dark we had no difficulty in finding spare-time amusement : there were always collections to sort out and catalogue – stamps, coins, cigarette cards, or whatever happened to be the fad of the moment. And sewing for me. Some boys were very clever at carpentry, and made all sorts of useful or ornamental (or frequently neither) constructions for their friends and relations to receive with appropriate admiration and gratitude. But carpentry was not a talent shared by Eric and Prosper. However, there were plenty of indoor games that we used to play. There were none of the complicated bought games like Monopoly or Cluedo, then, but we had Ludo, and Snakes and Ladders, as well as our favourite Halma. Chess we thought too serious, so the chessmen seldom left their box, and Tiddlywinks too childish, so they were used as counters in other games, together with farthings.

The Blairs had a very popular game called Winkle's Wedding, in which cards with well-described nouns printed on them were dealt out, face downward, and you must not look at them. Then an accompanying narrative with blanks in it was read by the player who represented the Master of Ceremonies, the blanks being filled in by the player-in-turn reading out his top card, whose inapposition was guaranteed by the brochure to cause roars of merriment.

Eg :

'The best man's present to the Groom was . . . .'
'A pair of old socks with holes in them'
or
'The Bride's mother trimmed her hat with . . . . .'
'A complete Crown Derby tea service'

Except for Happy Families, we had no specially-printed playing-cards for such games as Snap or Old Maid, as children do today. These were played with ordinary cards, and the Queen of Spades was Old Maid.

One excellent card-game had been taught us by our French Mademoiselle, Julienne Hue. It was called Nain Jaune, and certain diamonds were of prime importance, especially the seven – I can hear now the screams of triumph : *'Me voici le sept – le bon p'tit sept'* . . . and the king, *'Bon Roi!! Payez-moi! ! !'* Was it a French version of Pope Joan, perhaps?

Racing Demon was a firm favourite, and Guiny though young was phenomenally proficient. It was said of her that she could play with both hands, her feet, and her teeth. And one of Eric's specialities was Coon Can (I believe it should be spelt Kuhn Khan), a relative of Rummy and the more modern Canasta. Another game, chiefly preferred by Eric and Prosper, was Cheating: but I forget how it was played. I think that they invented its madly complicated rules themselves – they never seemed the same two games running.

Actual cheating was permissible in *any* game – so long as you could get away with it undiscovered. But if you were suspected and challenged, you were in honour bound to plead guilty. And the penalties were dire: sometimes 'out of the game altogether', at others such heavy fines on points that all chances of winning were lost.

We played a certain amount of Roulette, the equipment being given to us by Uncle Dudie, who considered no nursery complete without it. Before and after the War, he usually spent some time each winter at Monte Carlo, though he was *not*, as we children at one time imagined, *The Man who Broke the Bank* in the music-hall song taught us by Nors.

Games like Tag or Hide-and-seek we were by that time too old for, but there was a chasing game called You after Me that we played at Quarry House occasionally in the winter evenings – a sort of free-for-all, rushing after each other down the front stairs and up the back, hiding round corners and unexpectedly jumping out on the stragglers, with the lamplight flickering in the shadows of the passages. For some strange reason, though we knew the house and each other so well, it always seemed rather frightening.

Of course it was Eric who first made it scaring – he was often the originator of intriguing theories – by saying: 'How can you be sure I'm *me*? It's dark in the corners, and I might have been *got into* by the shadow of a shadow, and then when you came past I'd *pounce* – and you'd be the shadow of a shadow too – and we *mightn't be able to get back*!' But always chivalrous he did add: 'Don't tell the Little Ones.' And a good thing too: the shadow of a shadow sounded far more fearful than a shadow itself. I always imagined it as *looming* – very much larger – with not-quite hands, and not-quite claws: it was too shadowy to see.

4

Paper Games

WHEN NOT ENGAGED in other occupations, we played various writing and drawing games with pencils and paper. There were two general favourites, called by us the Ponsfords' Game (because it was originally shown us by some people called Ponsford) and Ladders (because that was its shape) though I believe both are known by other names elsewhere.

Ladders was played by picking a word of six letters (usually with eyes shut and a pin) which each player wrote down in a column, with the same word reversed on the opposite side of his page. For example, if PIGSTY were picked, write it:

```
P.............................Y
I.............................T
G.............................S
S.............................G
T.............................I
Y.............................P
```

Then, with a time limit of ten minutes, each player fills in his spaces with words beginning and ending with the given letters:

each in turn describing his word and the others guessing it. The first person to guess it correctly would score as many points as the word has syllables. If nobody could guess it correctly, the same number of points would go to the author. Therefore, the description, while having to be accurate, must not be too easy, and the longer the word the better.

One of my own best efforts, for C.........N was CIRCUM-NAVIGATION, 'Ending up where you started', which scored me seven points from everybody. But Eric went one better. A week or two later, C.........N turned up again, and Eric made a great song-and-dance something on these lines: 'Well, I don't really know exactly how to describe this. You wouldn't find it at Harrods or Selfridges – it isn't *new* – but I can't imagine you buying it at an *ordinary* second-hand dealers, or even a better-class pawnbroker. Certainly not on an old junk-barrow. But I think you can quite definitely say that it has been used before.' Nobody could guess this mysterious article of commerce, so Eric gleefully chalked up his multiplication of sevens, and we had to admit his description entirely accurate. His word? CIRCUMNAVIGATION, of course.

The Ponsfords' Game consisted of a dozen categories, one chosen by each player in turn, and written down in a column: as, RIVER, ISLAND, COUNTRY, TREE (from the aid-to-Latin rhyme), FAMOUS CRICKETER (Prosper), AUTHOR (Eric), BOOK (me), BIRD (Guiny), etc. Then a letter was picked (eyes shut and with a pin, and you could have three goes if the first letters were impossible or had been used too recently already) and a list of a word for each of the categories, beginning with that letter, written down in ten minutes, adding if possible not more than *three* appropriate adjectives, except for PEOPLE for whom alliterative or double-barrelled alliterative names counted. E.g. for VICE starting with S, 'sloth' would only count one point, but 'stealing small-sized sausages' would count four. That was one of Eric's: he pointed out that sausages would need to be small-sized to fit the pockets of that particular thief, who made such a habit of stealing them that it had become an *absolute* vice with him. I think there was a bit of an argument as to whether an *absolute* and original vice ought to count double-points in contrast to an occasional and common one: but the conclusion was that a vice was a vice whatever its inveteracy. (We remember such silly things in such detail, and the useful, important things get irretrievably buried in oblivion.)

Eric's most notorious victory in the Ponsfords' Game was when, for a tree beginning with T, he gave THE TUM TUM TREE and claimed four for it. Prosper said, 'I've never heard of a tum tum tree', which was a mistake. He should have said, '*I challenge*'. Eric allegedly took it that Prosper was just admitting ignorance so he exhibited vast contempt: 'Surely *everybody* must have heard of THE TUM TUM TREE. It isn't just *a* tum tum tree – it's the special *sacred* one – there's a full-page illustration in Doctor Mallinson's *African Explorer*. You *must* have heard of Doctor Mallinson!' We were all most suitably impressed, and Eric was agreed his claimed four. After the game was over, he delightedly divulged that not only was THE TUM TUM TREE deliberately concocted for the occasion, but that Dr. Mallinson, with the *African Explorer* as well, were equally products of his own imagination.

Eric and I, in general less active and more contemplative than the others, were more addicted to paper games than they were. Our own favourite was Set-Piece-Poetry, which we spent a lot of time playing together – it was ideal for two people. Prosper did not much care for poetry, and Guiny and Avril were both too young for fair competition. All three were more interested in the minor livestock, so when they were busy cleaning out rabbit-hutches, feeding the hens, and so on, Eric and I retired with our pencils and papers to peace.

Rules were fairly elastic, but decisions once made for any

given game had to be strictly kept. There was always a *set subject* : sometimes chosen by one of us in turn, sometimes one or more words picked (as usual with eyes shut and a pin) from a book, either for title or alternatively to be included in the poem. Length, within limits, was specified : otherwise the prolific Eric might have run into fifty cantos, and the lazy Jacintha might have stopped at four lines.

Metre and/or *system of rhyming* were sometimes, but not always, laid down, and *un-dictionary* (i.e. invented words) in various different competitions might be either *obligatory, to choice,* or *forbidden.* If too obvious, a penalty point was deducted, if undetected, a bonus point was awarded. Eric was pretty good at undictionary words : 'double-think' and 'newspeak' were by no means his first ventures in the field. They came at the end of a very long apprenticeship indeed : he was a *Britannian* right at the beginning of the First World War, and to prove it had two poems published in the *Henley and South Oxfordshire Standard*.

He was only eleven when he wrote the first, which appeared on 2 October 1914 :

Awake! Young Men of England

Oh! give me the strength of the Lion,
  The wisdom of Reynard the Fox
And then I'll hurl troops at the Germans
  And give them the hardest of knocks.

Oh! think of the War Lord's mailed fist,
  That is striking at England today:
And think of the lives that our soldiers
  Are fearlessly throwing away.

Awake! Oh you young men of England,
  For if, when your Country's in need,
You do not enlist by the thousand,
  You truly are cowards indeed.

Eric was pleased to see his work in print, but not quite so pleased at being described as '*Master* Eric Blair, the eleven-year-old son of Mr R W Blair'. Though his parents may have felt that his youth gave added credit to his prowess, Eric thought such personal information an unnecessary embellishment. How could he be classed by *his public* with all these brave soldiers himself, if they were told he was only eleven years old?

His second poem appeared on 21 July 1916, this time signed with simple dignity E A Blair. It was, I think, originally a school essay for St Cyprian's, on the death by drowning of Kitchener, which had occurred the previous month on 5 June:

Kitchener

No stone is set to mark his nation's loss,
No stately tomb enshrines his noble breast;
Not e'en the tribute of a wooden cross
    Can mark this hero's rest.

He needs them not, his name untarnished stands,
Remindful of the mighty deeds he worked,
Footprints of one, upon time's changeful sands,
    Who ne'er his duty shirked.

Who follows in his steps no danger shuns,
Nor stoops to conquer by a shameful deed,
An honest and unselfish race he runs,
    From fear and malice freed.

Both are typical *Britannian* poems: a Britannian was more than just a Briton, who might still be covered with woad. He was a *Rule Britannian*: England For Ever, and God Bless Our Glorious Empire, On Which May The Sun Never Set.

What *would* he have thought of it now?

With Prosper and Guiny, Eric was mostly involved in outdoor or sporting pursuits: with me, he *talked*. We both had independent minds with many ideas in common, and we shared a love for books. We were inveterate readers, and Eric had a vast vocabulary (our collective term) of volumes. It was a *vocabulary of volumes* for books read and talked about, and a *beatitude of books* for those actually possessed. He was always giving me books, lending me books, borrowing or exchanging books with me. He said that reading was good preparation for writing: *any* book could teach you something, if only how not to write one. Of course, Eric was always going to write: not merely as an author, always a FAMOUS AUTHOR, in capitals.

As a rule the etiquette was *not* to write dedicatory inscriptions in the books we gave each other, in case we wanted to exchange them with friends at school, or at the second-hand bookshop if we were particularly impecunious at that moment and needed something else more urgently. But he did write 'Jacintha from Eric' in a copy of *Manalive* by G K Chesterton that he gave me, because this was a book which he especially esteemed but thought I might not like at first sight, so he was determined it should be given a fair chance in the hope that I would 'get used to it' and in proof that there was another side to Chesterton besides the Father Brown stories which we both cherished. We had a passion for detective stories – as pure detection, not 'thrillers' – and on the whole preferred Thorndyke to Holmes, as Thorndyke was so usefully instructive and R Austin Freeman's inverted tales we thought more interesting than the ordinary 'don't know who dunnit till the last page'. Those days, alas, were all too early for Christie, Allingham, and Sayers, or for the Stewarts and Gilberts, for Dell Shannon who is Lesley Egan & Company, and such other moderns as delight the *aficionados*. (If any *aficionado* has not yet come across that admirable work by Eric's namesake, Dr Erik Routley, *The Puritan Pleasures of the Detective Story*, it will be a *red letter day* when he lights upon this page.)

Eric was a great admirer of Hornung, Conan Doyle's brother-in-law. He thought it rather nice for Holmes and Raffles to be in the same family. On the whole, he preferred Raffles to Holmes, and Stingaree to Raffles: but *my* favourite Hornung was *Witching Hill*. My own favourite detective story – and I'm not sure it isn't almost my favourite of any sort of story – is *The Daughter of Time* by Josephine Tey. That wasn't published till after Eric, and my mother, were dead. But *how* they would both have enjoyed it.

Eric's tastes in literature covered a wide range, but in our long discussions, his chief preference was for ghost stories. He was a great advocate for ghosts. One of his theories was that half the people in towns were ghosts: not so many in the country, where neighbours were better acquainted with each other, but in towns so many would be strangers anyway that we wouldn't know whether they were ghosts or not, if they walked about like anyone else. 'So *don't talk to strangers*, or you may get a ghost following after you.' He gave me *The Turn of the Screw*, and *The Room in the Tower* by E F Benson, among others, and introduced us to the works of M R James. I am surprised he did not publish a collection of Ghost Stories himself.

We had in our house a copy of Wells' *Modern Utopia*, belonging to RAB, who had known him, which was so greatly fancied by Eric that it was eventually given to him. He said he might write that kind of book himself. Broadly, *Nineteen Eighty Four* is classifiable as 'that kind of book'. And the genealogical tree of *Animal Farm* has its roots in *Pigling Bland*, by Beatrix Potter. *Pigling Bland* was Guiny's book: Eric and I were far too old for it, but we adored it all the same. I remember his reading it to me twice over from beginning to end, to cheer me up one time when I had a cold. And we used to call each other Pigling Bland and Pigwig in moments of frivolity. The heroic Pigling Bland was a white pig, and in *Animal Farm* the white pigs are the *good* pigs. But it is a sorry metamorphosis for the delicious Black Berkshire Pigwig to be replaced by the dreadful Black Berkshire Napoleon. Mr Pilkington in *Animal Farm* is a relative of Beatrix Potter's Mr Peter Thomas Piperson, I think.

On his list of 'best' short stories (*New Statesman*, 25 January 1941) I recognise his old favourites, Poe's *Premature Burial*, Kipling's *Baa Baa Black Sheep*, and Wells' *Slip under the Microscope*. I can testify to his obsession with *The Country of the Blind*: in a General Knowledge Paper he set me (another of his spare-time occupations) one question was: 'Distinguish between Medina Sidonia and Medina Serote', which, naturally, at the time I found very easy to answer.

Remembering the young Eric, his later inclusion of Joyce and Lawrence is rather a mystery to me. *Some* of Lawrence's short stories are good, but I found it very difficult to wade through such exercises as *Lady Chatterley's Lover* even in 1933, when it was brought to me by a current boy-friend with great *éclat* as a 'Present From Paris'. I returned it to him, suggesting politely that he might find it more useful for somebody else. Myself, I should have preferred a nice bottle of scent to the smells of the pheasant-coop. Most of Lawrence's novels seem to me messy, and Joyce's mad – there are better things to read than all this grubby garrulity: and I can't understand the meticulous Eric bothering with it either, except as an aftermath of his tramps. Oh well, a rose is a rose is a rose, even if it's only floating on a bandwagon.

In his later works Eric mentions several authors whose books he first met at Quarry House. Charles Reade, another of his twelve favourites (*Collected Essays*, Vol. ii, p 39), was also a favourite of my mother's – I was called Jacintha after a character in *The Double Marriage* – and she had a collected edition which Eric was constantly borrowing. According to its inscription, I gave her for her birthday, 25 July 1919, *The Twilight of the Gods*, by Richard Garnett. This had previously been recommended and lent to me by Eric: and he recommends it to Brenda Salkeld in September 1932, together with *Dr Nikola* by Guy Boothby, and *The Fairchild Family* – both familiar friends of our youth (*Collected Essays*, Vol i, pp. 125-6).

To Shakespeare and Dickens he remained faithful. Eric, Guiny, and I were all devoted to Shakespeare, and Guiny is often to be found reading him still. Eric used to write him: constantly concocting long historical dramas in blank verse, which he read aloud to me with different voices for the different parts. Gruff and manly for the heroes: alternatively ultra-plebeian or mincing la-di-dah for the villains: wheezing shakily for the greybeards. And a squealing falsetto for the female characters reminiscent of the trough at an overdue feeding-time, which often dissolved us both into such helpless giggles that Eric was unable to continue his recital. I once suggested that I should 'do the ladies', but Eric declined this well-meant offer: he would not allow his sacred screeds out of his own hands. I never *saw* these Masterpieces – he only read them to me – which is probably why I remember very little about their tortuously-complicated plots. I don't know why the *dramas* were so sacrosanct: he showed me plenty of other examples of his craft. There were, for example, a whole series of tales about a rather Barry-Paineish, mostly humorous, individual called *Mr Puffin*. And his very good ghost story, *The Lantern*.

But these came later, when he was at Eton. When first we knew him he was still at his prep school, St Cyprian's, Eastbourne.

5

Were Such the Joys?

On 31 May 1947, George Orwell wrote to his publisher and friend, Fredric Warburg:

> I am sending you separately a long autobiographical sketch which I originally undertook as a sort of pendant to Cyril Connolly's *Enemies of Promise*, he having asked me to write a reminiscence of the preparatory school we were at together. I haven't actually sent it to Connolly or *Horizon* because apart from being too long for a periodical, I think it is really too libellous to print and I am not disposed to change it except perhaps the names. But I think it should be printed later when the people most concerned are dead, and maybe sooner or later I might do a book of collected sketches.
>
> (*Collected Essays*, Vol IV, p 378)

This 'sketch', *Such Such were the Joys*, was tactfully published in the United States, with the school St Cyprian's called 'Crossgates': in both the American, and in the later English version, the names of schoolfellows and masters were changed.

The picture, painted mostly dun and grey with occasional highlights of polished black, is taken – with popping eyes and bated breath, by those who did not know him then – to be the most literal of fact: the Very Gospel according to Saint George. It would appear to be the basis of the *Orwell Mystique* that his whole life was blighted, his entire self-confidence destroyed, and all his emotional stability overthrown, by the desperate unhappiness of his childhood, and his fateful experiences at school.

It seems time for a little illumination to be turned on to this tenebrous scene.

To begin with, the sketch was originally described as 'a pendant to Cyril Connolly's *Enemies of Promise*'. Cyril Connolly had portrayed their mutual prep school in an unfavourable light, to say the least. So Eric went one better, to out-do Dotheboys Hall. He might of course, being Eric, have decided to take the opposite side and to depict St Cyprian's as Elysium piled on Arcadia. But he most likely would have thought that this might not be what Cyril Connolly would want, in a more or less commissioned article – the lie direct to the Connolly version: and Eric himself, writing at a time when he had already embarked on *Nineteen Eighty Four*, was doubtless not feeling very Arcadianly disposed. There is a recognisable dominant note echoing between these two contemporary Orwell works. It might seem not so much that *Nineteen Eighty Four* was inspired by life at St Cyprian's as that *Such Such were the Joys* was an apocryphal description of the sort of prep school exemplified in *Nineteen Eighty Four* by an obverse Big Brother.

Secondly, thirty years after Eric had left St Cyprian's in 1916, factual basis is deliberately channelled to selective remembrances, in which occasional particular instances are very much generalised. Devotees of the *Mystique* give no credit to Eric for any imagination or originality at all, either in this essay or in his novels. They assume that he is only able to write bald accounts of exactly what happened to *him*, with no invention or embellishment whatsoever. They seem oblivious to his penchant for unpoetic license.

43

I remember a letter he wrote Prosper from the crammers he went to, quoted and re-quoted by our family as typical of Eric: 'Millions of people at this crammers shoot – at least three of us'. His opinion that *Such Such were the Joys* was too libellous to print may well apply to acknowledged exaggeration rather than veracity.

Thirdly, the circumstances should be considered in the light of the times to which they refer, and not to the very much altered circumstances of today, or the different customs of other countries. So that for Eric to go to boarding-school at the age of eight was nothing singular: the singularity would have been if he had *not* done so. Unless lucky enough to live near a good preparatory day-school (and such schools were scarce) or unfortunate enough to have such poor health, or such a molly-coddling mother, that he was not allowed to leave home, nearly every middle-to-upper class boy was sent by then to prep school as a boarder.

Again, it would be nothing singular for a child most naturally to be homesick and unhappy at first, pitchforked at this tender age into a totally alien and regimented environment with a crowd of other boys – a necessarily Spartan contrast to the usually indulgent home where, if an only son especially, he would have previously been the favoured little king of a protective castle. Some boys, extrovert members of large families, accustomed to rough-and-tumble among several brothers and cousins, might settle down very quickly. Others, sensitive and reserved, or with little experience of their contemporaries, would take a good deal longer to adjust to the new surroundings. But little boys are hardy creatures who manage to adapt themselves to most circumstances that are required of them with reasonable success. And Eric was no exception. His first term or two may well have been extremely miserable: but by the time we knew him, and we knew him very well indeed, he had quite recovered. He was a philosophical boy, with varied interests and a sense of humour – which he was inclined to indulge when referring to St Cyprian's in the holidays.

I had not met him when he first arrived there in 1911, and as I never visited the school myself cannot speak at first hand as can Cyril Connolly. But what does Cyril Connolly say about it now? In his own essay *Such Were The Joys*:

> In the case of St Cyprian's and the Wilkes whom I had so blithely mocked there is an emotional disturbance. I received a letter of bitter reproach from Mrs Wilkes after *Enemies of Promise* which I have never dared to reread, and when, after the death of my own parents, their papers descended to me, I found evidence of the immense trouble she had taken to help me win my scholarship to Eton despite the misgivings of my father which had to be overcome. The Wilkeses were true friends, and I had caricatured their mannerisms, developed from dealing with generations of boys, and I had read mercenary motives into much that was just enthusiasm. What they would have made of Orwell's more severe strictures, published in England only after his death in 1950, I have no idea. I hope they never saw them. (*New York Times Book Review* of 12 November 1972)

For Eric's last seven or eight terms at St Cyprian's, we saw him nearly every day during most of the holidays, and subsequently throughout his time at Eton: and I can guarantee that the 'I' of *Such Such Were the Joys* is quite unrecognisable as Eric when we knew him then.

Take his description of himself (*Collected Essays*, Vol iv, pp 412-3):

> The schoolmasters with their canes, the millionaires with their Scottish castles, the athletes with their curly hair, these were the armies of unalterable law. It was not easy, at that date, to realise that in fact it *was* alterable. And according to that law I was damned. I had no money. I was weak. I was ugly. I was unpopular. I had a chronic cough. I was cowardly. I smelt. I was an unattractive boy. St Cyprian's soon made me so, even if I had not been so before . . . The conviction that it was *not possible* for me to be a success went deep enough to influence my actions till far into adult life.

Let us examine in their various details these *armies of un-alterable law.*

The schoolmasters with their canes: Prosper and Eric often talked about their respective prep schools, and my impression is that at neither school did very much caning go on: that, although masters had the privilege of canes, they seldom used them. At their public schools the masters' function was to teach – by precept and persuasion – while discipline and corporal punishment were more the province of the senior boys and public opinion. By the time Eric and Prosper reached their own sixth forms, there was a revulsion against its having been previously *over*done – I believe that at Eton the seniors prior to Eric's lot were notoriously excessive – so that caning was emphatically *not the done thing.* If it is said that Eric never beat *anybody,* I can well credit it. Prosper was very angry indeed with the one Harrovian juvenile delinquent whose delinquency was such that Prosper was *obliged* to beat him: this anger being caused not by the actual wickedness itself but because the culprit had thereby *broken Prosper's record* of never having to use the cane.

The millionaires with their Scottish castles: Surely a most mini-minority? In a contemporary letter, would Eric have appended 'Both of them'? But I think that somehow the rich and Scottish had terrific appeal for Mrs Wilkes, of whom I remember Eric saying something like, 'To be a favourite with old Mum you have to be a Duke in a Kilt.' But this was at the time considered as a sidesplitting joke rather than a subject for aggrieved envy.

The athletes with their curly hair: Eric's own hair was as straight as bootlaces, so doubtless he didn't admire it. Prosper's hair was very fair and curly, and Prosper at his prep school was quite athletic – he loved games – but he thought his own curls so undesirable that he constantly but ineffectually plastered them with water to flatten them down. I don't remember Eric advising him to desist on the grounds that curly hair was an advantage. Nor do I recall Eric suffering any attacks of hero-worship for the cricketing and footballing bloods. Armies of unalterable law these might have been, but to the irreverent schoolboy Eric they were lumped together as lesser gods *without* the law : he so much preferred brain to brawn. One might as well expect Bertrand Russell to wave a whistling rattle at Georgie Best. But of course Eric would not have told the other boys that : one must inhabit Rome with the Romans.

According to Prosper (it was not a subject he would have discussed with me) Eric had no homosexual tendencies : so that although on the one hand he may not have attracted overtures because he was 'decidedly not pretty' (Malcolm Muggeridge, introduction to *Burmese Days*, quoting Cyril Connolly) on the other hand, he made no collection of 'pretty boys' himself.

I had no money: Though far removed from the Scottish Millionaire class, *in the holidays* Eric always seemed to have sufficient funds for the usual little treats as well as essentials, certainly as much as we had. And at prep schools in those days boys did not have an unlimited amount of money, nor did they need it. The modern child, even the modern young parent, may not realise that the current fashion of spoonfeeding with fantastically extravagant and expensive toys was then unheard of. Today, little girls' dolls have an unlimited choice of marvellous outfits each costing nearly as much as the child's own clothes, and competition is keen. If Janey Jones's Sindy has seventeen sets – all complete with hats and handbags – then Betsy Brown simply *must* have another to equal her. In our young day, we girls made our own dolls' clothes, which gave us far more sense of real achievement after a bit of time and trouble, and at least incidentally taught us which end to thread a needle. And for boys it was the same sort of thing : they made their own models and had constructive hobbies and collections which cost very little. At Prosper's school a specific sum for pocket-money was laid down, neither more nor less, per term. If Eric had really required extra cash for anything, I am sure that his quite indulgent mother would have given it to him in termtime as readily as she did in the holidays, even if he did not care to try his less-approachable father.

So long as we had enough to supply our quite reasonable and moderate tastes – and we were willing to save up and wait for something special – money was not important to us. It *did not matter*, any more than pompous circumstance mattered. Beachcomber's Sir Hardleigh Heumann might have a far finer house than ours, but we took it for granted that some people did: and if his son was a little beast, then we discouraged him as a little beast – we did not toady to him in the hope of bigger helpings of strawberries and cream. Conversely, if Mr Goodheart had a smaller house than ours, again we took it as a matter of course and not as an excuse to put on side ourselves: if his son was a kind and clever boy, we valued him extremely and thought ourselves lucky to be his friends. When we were young, I do not think we were affected at all by worldly position: we did not try to keep up with the Joneses because we simply did not realise that there was any reason for the Joneses to *be* kept up with. People were themselves, not what they arbitrarily had, and that was that. I suppose we were democrats.

Where Eton finances were concerned, it must be remembered that although plenty of plutocrats are to be found there, Eric was by no means the sole, single, solitary pauper. As a King's Scholar he was only one among seventy, many of whom would have come from equivalent financial and social backgrounds. Moreover, since Eton is in many cases a family tradition, among the Oppidans there would have been *some* boys in more stringent straits: if they were not clever enough to gain scholarships, it would have meant further financial sacrifice if their fathers were not well-off but still had to find the full fees for their sons to be educated at their old school.

In *The Unknown Orwell* (p 76) Stansky and Abrahams recount an anecdote:

> Once, when he had been home on a visit (to Mall Chambers) Marjorie Blair had to borrow money from Ruth Pitter for Eric's ticket back to Eton. That was on a Sunday, and the next day, when the banks were open, the loan was repaid. But by then Eric had gone, and the need to have borrowed so small a sum of money must have left its impression upon a nature abnormally sensitive to such things.

This does not impress me as proving either the desperate poverty of the Blairs, nor the infliction of an ineradicable scar on the sensitive Eric's soul. It was a *Sunday* evening, which brings to my mind having heard long ago presumably the same incident from Marjorie's point of view: 'How tiresomely typical of Eric to fail to let her know he had *not* come with the usual weekend-return ticket until *after* they had spent all their available cash in general junketing, going to a cinema or something: so that borrowing from a neighbour was a brainwave solution.' The Blair parents, as far as I remember, were absent.

It is parallel with an episode a few years later when Prosper and I were sharing a flat in Chelsea, on another Sunday evening, when the gas-fire suddenly expired. We were entertaining two or three friends, but nobody was able to provide another shilling for the meter. So Prosper braved the wild and rainy night in the Kings Road – it was after closing-time – and eventually found an elderly man with an umbrella, whom he asked to be kind enough to give him a shilling. He received in reply a virtuous speech, being complimented on looking at least clean and tidy though penniless, ending, 'Here's half-a-crown for you, my boy.' Prosper grumbled ungratefully, 'I don't want half-a-crown, I want a shilling', and, after expostulation and explanation, the man (who hadn't got one either) accompanied him to another passer-by who fortunately produced the essential coin, and both came back with Prosper to have a drink at the party.

I was weak, I was ugly, I was cowardly, I was an unattractive boy: I don't think he was particularly weak physically (except for the inherent delicacy of his chest: the chronic cough apparently noticed by our aunt for the first time in 1917, but never mentioned by his own mother in contemporary letters to ours. She worries about Avril's health, but says nothing about Eric). Of course older, larger boys would have been stronger by size and weight relative to age. He never seemed weak regarding endurance, nor collapsed from exhaustion before the rest of us: on the contrary, he was apparently seldom tired. He was hardly puny: in photos of 1917, he towers over Prosper, only a year younger, who was not a noticeably tiny child and eventually reached the average height of 5 feet 10 inches – but Eric was over six feet tall, long before he left Eton. Nor would *weak* be an appropriate character description of this inveterate individualist, who always thought for himself, and never ran with the crowd just because the crowd was running. He was certainly not at all cowardly: his unfailing kindness and chivalry to smaller children and those in a less advantageous position surely came from strength, not weakness. He could not fairly have been called ugly and unattractive: though not specially handsome, and in his early years rather chubby, he was quite a reasonably decent-looking boy, improving as he grew older and taller and slimmer.

I was unpopular: A fat lot the self-sufficient, self-contained, supercilious Eric would have cared whether he was *popular* or not. What he thought, he thought: what he did, he did – without being *interested* in whether he was liked or disliked for it, or what effect he was creating. Effects were doubtless created, but they were by-products, and not objectives. It would be really more accurate to say that the other people were unpopular with *him*. I do not think that this was in the least 'sour grapes', any renouncing of his fellows because they had discarded *him*: he was not a gregarious person with the genuine herd-instinct. His whole life seems to have proved this. True, at times he tried to make himself so, as in the Tramp Period, but these attempts were never much of a success. Perhaps he picked the wrong herds.

I smelt: If he had really smelt, I for one would never have associated with him – I did not associate with the rabbits and the chickens, or even *Aw-pig*.

But since people aren't supposed to be able to smell themselves unless their best friends tell them, 'I' must have deduced that he smelt, from smelling the other boys. In which case, at school, his nose may not have been far wrong. It is simple fact that through a good deal of his schooldays there was a war on, with the consequent shortage of amenities – food, soap, fuel, and service among them: the maids had patriotically gone off to make munitions at much more money.

My own recollections of school food in wartime are that it was unspeakable. Never the so-much-preferable potatoes – there was a severe potato shortage – only hitherto unheard-of cereals that we wished we hadn't been obliged to hear of then. Instead of meat, some horrid sort of substitute sausage demonstrably made of gristle and sawdust. And porridge – *porridge* – *PORRIDGE* – till oats grew out of our ears.

School washing-up, with inadequate domestic staff, also left much to be desired. Eric complained of dirty fork-prongs: I, at school, always cleaned my fork on my table-napkin before using it, and when eventually table-napkins were soap-shortaged out of existence, I carried two pocket-handkerchiefs: the one under my right-leg knicker-elastic to blow my nose on, the left one for cleaning forks, cups, or whatever else needed it. Nevertheless, gourmet as I am and always was from the day of my two-candled birthday-cake, I *loved* school.

Baths were curtailed everywhere. Like Eric, we too only had

one hot bath a week, but it *was* a bath each and not communal. And of course girls are not in general so active as boys, so there was less occasion for nasal notice. If a crowd of boys have to play energetic, sweaty, and often muddy games with abbreviated facilities – cold showers with insufficient soap, and inadequate cleaning and laundering of their clothes, naturally they will smell.

It is on a par with the famous *Orwell Dictum* that *the working classes smelt.* Wherever proper washing facilities are absent, whenever work is heavy manual labour – like the boys' games, energetic, sweaty, and dirty – and when clothing is perforce too infrequently changed, how could anyone escape possession of an odour? Nowadays when most homes have constant hot water and washing-machines, or fair proximity to the lavish launderette, and when the telly bombards us with advertisements for detergents and deodorants, it is easier for the possibility of *pong* to be perceived and prevented. But once upon a time, with only a pump in the common yard or a tap in the washhouse, and *The Specialist*'s specialism at the bottom of the garden: with six-in-a-bed and wages insufficient to give big families even *one* square meal a day, or clothe them all except from cast-offs or jumble sales, life was not so easy. *Cleanliness is next to Godliness:* Godliness, costing only prayers and goodwill, they might possess in abundance, but difficult and expensive cleanliness in the towns of the earlier machine-age had to come next at considerable distance.

The conviction that it was not possible for me to be a success went deep enough to influence my actions till far into adult life: Now why should 'I' feel deeply convinced that it was not possible to be a success? In accord with the ambitions of his parents and masters, with which he was then inevitably preoccupied, his own success had been overwhelming. The wish to achieve a scholarship had been doubly granted: he had obtained not one, but two – the choice of Eton or Wellington, with actual entry to *both* schools. So how can blame be attached either to himself as a *failure*, or to poor old St Cyprian's, so proudly pleased with him that the whole school was given a day's holiday to celebrate his academic prowess?

He had, *at that time*, reached an enviable summit. He had acquired the reputation of being the school's *best poet*: a distinction he valued far more than he would have valued the reputation of being *best at games*: 'any fool can play games' (Eric to me *circa* 1916 or 1917). He had made at least one loyal friend, whose friendship lasted the rest of his life. No. Disillusionment came later. In *Such Such Were the Joys* we hear the voice of the sick and disappointed man of forty-three: not the voice of the good-humoured cynic schoolboy of fourteen.

It may sometimes seem desirable for a scapegoat to be selected: perhaps poor old St Cyprian's was Eric's.

6

Postscript to the Joys

FOR PRACTICAL PURPOSES, Eric may have been said to have left
St Cyprian's in a virtual blaze of glory. But the beginning of
his sojourn there was less auspicious. He opens his account:

> Soon after I arrived at St Cyprian's, (not immediately, but
> after a week or two, just when I seemed to be settling into
> the routine of school life) I began wetting my bed. Nowadays
> I believe bed-wetting in such circumstances is taken for
> granted. It is normal reaction in children who have been re-
> moved from their homes to a strange place. In those days,
> however, it was looked on as a disgusting crime which the
> child had committed on purpose and for which the proper
> cure was a beating.

This makes an arresting beginning, especially in 1947 when
literary, as against medical, discussion of eneuresis was still
something of a novelty: in permissive 1973 it would be very
mild run-of-the-mill. Of course it was not an anecdote he would
ever have recounted to me post-1914. Not so much that it
verged on the vulgar, but simply that we would have thought
it boring: What *possible* interest could we have found in an

excessively brief childish tendency which had at best lasted only a week or two, and which was over and finished and done-with years ago?

Anyway, after a couple of misguided beatings, the short-lived phase ceased: and I should imagine that until he decided it would make an effective opening sentence, it had barely crossed his mind again. He was not a boy to ruminate over trifles, magnifying them out of all proportion: and if the devotees of the *Mystique* claim that he must have been brooding about it in secret without ever ceasing for a moment, then they did not know Eric.

To anyone who did know him, his later corollary on this same subject in this same essay is of more interest than the episode itself. He says (*Collected Essays*, Vol iv, p 418):

> Here is a case, not known to me personally, but known to someone I can vouch for and happening within my own life-time. A small girl, daughter of a clergyman, continued wetting her bed at an age when she should have grown out of it. In order to punish her for this dreadful deed, her father took her to a large garden-party and there introduced her to the whole company as a little girl who wetted her bed: and to under-line her wickedness he had previously painted her face black.

We observe that this curious conduct is not acknowledged personally by Eric himself, only 'known' to someone unspeci-fied he 'can vouch for'. Of course, the someone might have been less vouchable than Eric imagined, but it seems to me the purest possible Doctor Mallinson.

Granted that some (also unspecified) clergyman might be so un-Christian and such an unkind father as to wish to exhibit his little daughter, with a blacked face, as an inveterate bed-wetter, surely mere expediency would deter him from actually doing so. In the Edwardian/George VI era – Eric's lifetime – bed-wetting was simply *not* a subject for garden-party conver-sation: the conventional elderly ladies of the parish would *not* have been amused. And it is on the conventional elderly ladies of a parish (great frequenters of each other's garden-parties) that a clergyman most depends for help in running the various parish activities, and for the higher offerings upon the plate. If it had been his own parish, he would have damned himself rather than his little daughter: if it had been anyone else's, his extraordinary behaviour would have put him quite beyond the pale. In either case, he would never have been tolerated at any garden-party ever again. Even in permissive 1974 it sounds peculiarly unpermissible – he was supposed to be a *clergyman*, not a beatnik exhibitionist: there still are plenty of wealthy elderly – and younger – ladies who do not take kindly to gratuitous embarrassment, and those good-natured young men who remain to do voluntary church work could well, in sympathy for the unhappy child, be even more disapproving.

It might appear that that particular 'garden-party' most probably took place under the shade of The Tum Tum Tree.

7

Nineteen Seventeen: Ticklerton

ERIC LEFT ST Cyprian's just before Christmas 1916, at the end of the autumn term. He spent the following spring term at Wellington, and was very glad that his sojourn lasted no longer. Having had a taste of freedom in his last months at St Cyprian's with the intensive scholarship work behind him, he expected a Public School to open the door to a wider world. So the Spartan, military Wellington, run somewhat on the lines of the well disciplined Winchester, was a cold-douche disappointment to him.

But by good fortune he was not committed to Wellington beyond this one term, and in May 1917 – a few weeks before his fourteenth birthday – he was able to take up the place now available for him at Eton. I am indebted to Cyril Connolly for explaining to me that the reason he had to wait to get to Eton was that only a dozen or so scholars were admitted at a time, according to the vacancies as older boys left: Eric, though he was successful in achieving his scholarship, was only fourteenth on the list.

The atmosphere of Eton was entirely different from that of Wellington, and Eric, good at swimming, took to it as a duck to water. The overall impression I got from him regarding his various schools was that he was indifferent to St Cyprian's, that he thought Wellington was beastly, and that he was interested and happy at Eton. At any rate, he gave us very favourable accounts when we saw him in the summer holidays of 1917.

He spent part of these summer holidays, with Prosper and Guiny, at our Buddicom Grandfather's home in Shropshire. When we were considered old enough to take the journey unescorted, we used to go up to Ticklerton for a week or more nearly every holidays: sometimes Prosper and me, sometimes Prosper and Guiny, sometimes all three of us, and on many occasions we were accompanied by Eric. I think he went with Prosper and me during the 1917 Easter holidays, and that that may have been one of the occasions when we ensured a carriage to ourselves by Eric asking Prosper very loudly whether his *spots* had come out yet. Once, when this had no effect, he swung from the luggage-rack, scratching himself and declaring he was an orang-outang: which was overdoing it, because the Surplus Lady-passenger only exclaimed that she would 'call the guard if you don't get down at once, you naughty boy!' I expect most children play these well-worn tricks. The journey to Shropshire was a popular one: the train always stopped at Banbury, where an attendant walked up and down the platform with Banbury cakes for sale. Straight from the oven, flaky, buttery, and curranty, could anything have been more delicious for travelling children? Or any traveller, for that matter.

For the 1917 summer holidays there is an informative letter from our Aunt, Lilian Buddicom, to our mother:

> Ticklerton Court
> Church Stretton
> Aug 29/17

Dearest Laura
Thank you for your letter. I did not write yesterday because Prosper had wired.

We will take all possible care over the shooting. It is a single-barrelled gun, so there is not the risk of a boy firing off a *second* barrel while the other is running forward to pick up the game, & Ted keeps the cartridges in his pocket, only handing out one at a time. [*Ted was Ted Hall, the Estate Man who acted as keeper.*] Prosper has never been allowed to take a gun out alone, & to be on the safe side I keep all the cartridges locked up! The only further precaution we could take would be to send one boy out at a time, but they would not enjoy it so much. They went out almost directly after they arrived yesterday, with Ted – the two boys. He would not take Guinever & I was very relieved. I could go too, but if we go 5 probably no rabbits would be shot – Prosper shot 3 rabbits, & Eric one with his second shot, which I think was very good as he has never shot before. Poor Guinever looked *very* sad to be left behind, specially as she was probably feeling a little strange. She seems such a good, quiet child. They have all been out for a walk together, & now they are at the pool together with Father, & *perhaps* some perch will arrive. [*Inserted later*] They have caught 4.

The Tennis ground is too wet to mow, let alone play tennis on. I hope the weather will improve. It is tolerably fine now, but it *poured* all night, & everything is saturated & impossible for the boys to tramp through the turnips after partridges. They would get *soaked*.

We are so pleased to have them here & they seem such great friends.

Eric has a bit of a cough. He says it is chronic. *Is this really the case?* I don't remember it before.

I don't think Prosper looks so well as he did at Easter. I wonder if he gets enough food – I mean of course at Mr. Phillips, not at home. [*Mr. Phillips was the headmaster of Prosper's prep school.*] Couldn't your mother have him out oftener & give him a good substantial meat tea? I expect Sunday is the one day in the week when they have a good dinner at school. I would *send* Prosper food, but it is no use if it is divided through the school. And perhaps he is growing.

I think our sugar will allow us to have it on the table, as I have managed to get a little extra this week . . . your idea of substituting the savoury for a pudding once a day is a very good one as it saves the sugar. We always now have soup in the evening and I am getting quite clever at making soup out of vegetables, fragments of gravy, etc : left over . . .

I expect Sinsie is having an awfully happy time *alone* with you. I always used to simply love being alone with Mother. I hope you don't miss your other two too dreadfully.

Yrs with love
Lilian.

One reason why The Old Ride was chosen as Prosper's prep school was that, at Branksome Park, it was not far from Gran Finlay at Bournemouth. But of course that was before the War, during which she was so tied up with Red Cross work that she seldom had time for Prosper (or me when I was at Redmoor) to visit her.

Agricultural Shropshire suffered no real food shortage through either war. The farmers grew their own corn and baked their own bread – the rent of one of the farms was always partly paid, at Ticklerton, in a certain number of their delicious home-produced loaves every week. Fruit and vegetables were plentiful, so were hens, ducks, geese, and turkeys, with their respective eggs : and the cows were lavish with milk, cream, and butter. Somebody was always killing a pig, or a sufficiently fatted calf, or elderly sheep, and there were freshwater fish in the pools and rivers.

The account of Eric's first shooting is interesting. Prosper was not allowed to shoot until he was twelve, which age he would have attained the previous year. I don't know why Guiny had permission so much younger. Interesting also, is the fact that Eric's *chronic cough* was noticeable, even then. Guiny and I both remember that he was ill with pneumonia while he was at Eton.

There are two photographs of the Ticklerton summer holidays of that period, marked on the backs by Grandpa: 'W S Buddicom September 1917'. One shows the three children ready to go out shooting, taken in the stableyard, but it is a bit muzzy : their faces are screwed up as if they had the sun in their eyes, and perhaps Grandpapa's hand had shaken – he was seventy-seven then. The other is much clearer, and shows the three on the croquet-lawn, all wearing *boots*. So perhaps the grass, which looks rather long, was still too damp for mowing. It is *exactly* like Eric at that age – the happy, smiling schoolboy, with his happy, smiling friends. Eric would have been fourteen, Prosper thirteen, and Guiny ten.

Since Eric stayed several times at Ticklerton and seemed always particularly to enjoy his visits there, some description of the environment is appropriate.

Grandpapa, a widower, lived with his only daughter, Lilian, to keep house for him : both were congenial to Eric in different ways. Grandpapa did not shoot, after a long-ago accident in a dog-cart when he lost an eye, but was a very keen fisherman who gladly helped the young enthusiasts with their groundwork. One of the first things the boys always did when they got up there, in the evenings, was to catch up on the back numbers of the *Fishing Gazette* which had accumulated since their last visit, and to hear of any special trophies from the fishing holidays which Grandpapa took in Wales and Scotland from time to time.

Auntie Lilian was very knowledgeable in both natural and ordinary history, archaeology, and botany, and the byways and bygones of Shropshire in general. Any questions on flora, fauna, fossils, or local legends, she was usually able to answer : on the very rare occasions when she was baffled, her great friend, Miss Auden, with an even better memory, would be pretty sure to help. Miss Auden, courtesy-called 'Aunt Nettie' (she had the pretty name of Henrietta) kept house for *her* aged and reverend father in nearby Church Stretton. I visited her whenever possible : she had a treasure trove of interesting books, relics, and information. She was real aunt to the illustrious Wystan, but I cannot claim acquaintance with this celebrity. There is a Ticklerton photo of *circa* 1913 or 1914 with Prosper and me and a grown-up who *looks* very much like Miss Auden with two little boys – evidently younger as they are wearing sailor suits and Prosper is in schoolboy outfit. These *might* be little Auden boys staying with their grandfather : if not, I don't know who they could be, as any other *pair* of boys about that age whom we knew had sisters – who would surely have been present too, to play with me. The Horne boys, Kenneth and Ronald, would certainly have been accompanied by Ruth, and Joan who was a great friend of mine – slightly senior to me, and also at the Oxford High School : while the Clegg, Gatehouse, and McClintock boys – several older than me – would certainly not have been young enough to wear sailor suits.

Auntie Lilian used to take us to places of local interest on expeditions : there were numerous interesting castles (Stokesay was my favourite, though I think the boys preferred the large and ruinous Ludlow) and abbeys such as Buildwas and Wenlock, among others, where we often had picnics on sunny days, with special sandwiches according to our preferences. She was a splendid sort of aunt to have : entertaining and informative without being in any way pedantic or bossy, and with – I see now – a sincere devotion to her brother's children.

Ticklerton was a small estate with half-a-dozen or so farms, various cottages, the universally-providing village shop, and in those days a blacksmith – a necessity in great demand. The nearest town and main line station was Church Stretton, nearly four miles away. The house, Ticklerton Court, was a mixture : the vast expanse of cellars and the back were Elizabethan (stone, not timbered) but the east front, with a lovely Japonica, and the south side, with various creepers, had been refaced in the early nineteenth century and were, I thought, very ugly. There was an infinitely more attractive old Tudor Lower House Farm on the estate, just down the road and across the brook, which I always wished our family had lived in instead. But they mistakenly imagined 'The Court' to be *grander*.

It had about ten bedrooms, and there were three main sitting-rooms on the ground floor: drawing-room, dining-room, and library. All round the dining-room walls, and in every available space in the halls and passages, were case upon case of stuffed birds – of which we had what was alleged to be one of the best private collections in England: it had formerly included a Great Auk, but this was sold by a forebear before our day. These birds were a great inspiration to Prosper, Guiny, and Eric, all three devotees of ornithology.

Besides these main rooms were, on the ground floor, a very small smoking-room – disused after the death of Grandmama in 1914, whereupon Grandpapa became Master of his own domain and could permit himself to smoke wherever he chose – and a bigger square room where guns and fishing-rods were kept. Shooting in season took place over most of the estate and there were always rabbits to be kept down, and there were several pools with a few trout (before they were restocked and multiplied inordinately) and a lot of perch (not bad eating) as well as eels. Grandpapa had once seen an army of eels slithering down the meadows to the pool in front of the house, and Prosper and Eric hoped to repeat this memorable experience, but were never lucky enough to glimpse them.

On the top floor were two more large square rooms, facing south and protected by a gate, which were originally nurseries. RAB's was in red, and Auntie Lilian's in pale blue with a doll's house which was my delight: but Guiny, who preferred the boys' games, never played with it. It must have been fairly old, because it was in the house long before Auntie Lilian and, as Grandpapa had no sisters, must have belonged to the previous generation.

In 1917 the Blue Room was 'Auntie Lilian's sitting-room', but it later became a spare bedroom: our mother, put to sleep there once, complained of the Wraiths on the lawn visible from its window. The Red Room was turned into a study for 'Uncle John Hayward', who gave up his own house and came to live at Ticklerton when he married Auntie Lilian in 1918. He brought a lot of his old notepaper with him – such notepaper as I have never seen before or since, about a foot square and nearly as thick as cardboard, embossed Quorn Place, Loughborough, which made splendid drawing paper. He also brought some of his own furniture which was better than some of the Ticklerton furniture : great-grandfather Buddicom had cleared out most of the nice old oak and replaced it with mid-Victorian enormities (in every sense), but RAB retrieved one of two antique chests from the stables and granaries where they had been used for keeping tools and corn.

RAB had turned a little room next to his own old nursery into a *Museum Room*, full of alluring objects, among them some skeletons from the prehistoric Cornish burial-ground whose skulls were complete with teeth of miraculous preservation. When I was much younger I sometimes took out these remarkable teeth and put them back again, very bold and carefree on a sunny morning. But in bed at night I would wake in horrific fear that perhaps I had put them back in the wrong places, and that the skeletons would *come after me* in the dark, all phosphorescent, in gibbering indignation.

There was an enormous atticky room on this top floor on the west, called The Laundry, with boxes of absorbing clothes and books and odds-and-ends, besides a mass of attics proper above, under the roof. But I never dared to explore them : they had *spiders*. They had probably a great many unappreciated treasures as well, and I wish now that I had been braver, or more curious.

Downstairs was a further collection of kitchen, scullery, pantry, larders, and storerooms. But in 1917 there was no bathroom : only an upstairs loo on the first floor, with a highly-polished mahogany seat as big as a table, stretching from wall to wall, inset with a still-brighter polished pull-up brass handle and a very elaborately-patterned blue-and-white china pan that nowadays would probably be worth its weight in gold. Next to the loo was a tiny room (the first you came to along the corridor of the back staircase) which was *discovered by* RAB when he took measurements of the house which did not seem to tally. Its door had been papered over and RAB demanded that it should be unblocked and opened. Grandmama demurred, saying someone might have been infectiously ill there – though there was no such tradition. But RAB persevered and the room was found to be quite empty, and nobody caught anything. Eric was most intrigued by this story, and one time he and I – probably in the 1917 Easter holidays – went round measuring the rest of the house for hidden spaces. We decided that there might well be one beside the dining-room fireplace, where there was only a straight wall, whereas the rooms on both floors above it had big clothes-cupboards. But Grandpapa and Auntie Lilian were not impressed by our calculations, and rather unsportingly refused to have the wall taken to pieces to see if we were right.

RAB's 'secret room', conveniently situated above the pantry, was turned into a bathroom after Auntie Lilian married Uncle John, who also insisted on a men's cloakroom being added near the room with the guns. Before that, the *Gents* only had a very primitive out-of-doors arrangement round a shrubbery. And for baths we all had hip-baths in our bedrooms – some with high backs, the most sought-after, and some just round and shallow: but all had cans of hot water brought up from the scullery copper. These cans were of polished brass for grown-ups and visitors, and of tin painted brown for children. It was a landmark for me when, at fifteen or so, I was given grown-up visitor status with the prettiest of all the polished brass cans. It may seem strange for this state of affairs to last almost till 1920, but Salop was always about fifty years behind the times. There was no electricity till the mid 1930s: instead, a row of silver candlesticks set out on the oak chest in the hall for each person to take their allotted one up to their bedrooms where more, standing, candlesticks stood either side of the dressing-table looking glasses. You *never* had *lamps* in your bedroom, though lighting otherwise was by oil-lamps, with candelabra on the dining-table for dinner. (At Shiplake, though we still had lamps and candles till the mid-1920s – a decade before Ticklerton – at least bathrooms were included when the houses were built.) Some of the Ticklerton lamps were very attractive.

The end north rooms on the top floor were maids' rooms, but the middle room of the east front – entered from the back-stairs corridor – was another spare bedroom. It was a very pleasant, square, low room, with cabinets containing some of the surplus best china too good to use, and charming water-colours. It was inhabited only when all the other rooms were occupied, but most of us slept in it at some time or another. Eric, I think, was the first to start the hare that it was haunted – which Auntie Lilian strenuously denied. But most of us were pretty convinced. There was nothing in the least eerie about this rather attractive room, which I liked to sleep in because it got the morning sun. Nobody ever actually *saw* or *heard* anything: but we all had exactly the same absolute conviction that we had been suddenly woken up by somebody coming into, or going out of the room. We always thought it was a real person and only discovered at breakfast time that the accused imagined culprit had been innocent.

When I had this experience, I had taken up to bed a book I had brought with me which Auntie Lilian wanted to read, and on waking up with the impression of this just-departed presence I lit a match to see if she had come to take it while I was asleep. But she had not: when asked, she – and all the others – denied they had been there. Eric, on a previous occas-

ion, thought it had been Prosper waking him early to go fishing – but found himself alone in the still pitch darkness and
the middle of the night. Prosper, some years later, was positive
that it had been our mother, who suffered from insomnia and
did sometimes while away the lengthy hours by prowling
round to see if anyone was awake and inclined for conversation – but this time she had *not*.

Even Nors, as set against ghosts as Auntie Lilian, was not
immune. Many years later we were all living at Ticklerton in
her absence. Aunt Lilian had gone on a trip to Germany, leaving our mother in charge of the household and me in charge
of the cat – rather inappropriately named Leo as he was a dark
tabby striped more like a tiger. One morning Nors came down
to breakfast very cross with me: 'Why had I left the cat to
roam about pushing open his door and waking him up instead
of looking after it properly?' In fact, the cat had been with me
in my bedroom with the door shut and there was no possibility
that it, or any other cat, could have got into any other part of
the house.

Besides this 'haunted bedroom', there must have been something peculiar about the back stairs. Guiny's usual room was
the middle west bedroom on the back corridor of the first
floor. That summer she had to stay in bed for two or three
weeks because her heart had gone wrong again. The Old English Sheepdog, Bob, was very fond of her, and spent a lot of
time in her room or lying in the passage 'on guard' outside
her door. But to get there, he would never negotiate the back
stairs which were directly outside her door. Instead he always
went the long way round: to the end of the passage, through
the door to the upstairs hall, sliding and slithering on the highly
polished oak front stairs and front hall, through the downstairs
swing-door to the back corridor and along it to get out by the
kitchen door – almost directly below where he first started.
He went up the same way in reverse. At first we imagined he

might have had a fall on the back stairs – unlikely as they were plain scrubbed wood, and he had so many falls on the slippery oak in the front of the house that it should have given him a greater aversion. But nothing would alter his routine: if one of us took the backstairs short cut, calling Bob to accompany us, he would get up and painstakingly make his front-stair journey to meet us at the other end. Eventually we came to the conclusion that Bob believed the back stairs were haunted: but I wonder why we never tried to test him with the 'haunted bedroom'? It could not have been Bob who so disturbed Nors: he was put out in his kennel at night. This was in 1934, a far cry from Eric's theory of, probably, Easter 1917.

Concerning the Christmas holidays of 1917, we have a letter from Mrs Blair. By that time Mr Blair was Lieut Blair in the Army, and Marjorie was also doing war-work. So 36 St Marks Road had been let furnished and Mrs Blair had moved to London as a more convenient base for her own Ministry Work, and incidentally more profitable, since good rents were then obtainable for houses in Henley: London was less popular, with the Zeppelin scare. She started in a furnished room or bed-sitter at Earls Court, but the following year took a tiny flat in Mall Chambers, Notting Hill Gate. She writes to our mother in 1917:

23 Cromwell Crescent
Earls Court
S.W.5
Nov 14th 1917

My dear Mrs. Buddicom

I am writing to ask a *great* favour of you, which I hope you will not hestitate to refuse if you cannot see your way to doing it for me. I want to know if you will be so very kind as to have Eric and Avril for their Xmas holidays as paying guests? I am very awkwardly placed; as you know, my husband is in France, I am working up here, & our house is let till the end of January! I wrote to my sister-in-law to ask her if she would have the children & she was quite willing to do so, but she is only in rooms & the people where she is will not have any more children in the house. I feel it is most dreadfully cool of me asking you this, but these are such extraordinary times that one is forced to do out-of-the-way things, & as you have children of your own and have always been so very kind to mine, I felt I *could* ask you, but I will quite understand if you don't feel you can manage with 2 extra in your house, or if you will not have room for them. I do hope you won't think this proposal of mine too dreadfully cool & if you think you *can* have them will you let me know, about terms etc & do try to forgive my seeming coolness. I hope you are well & have good news of Jacintha & Prosper.

Yours very sincerely
Ida Blair

There is no further existing correspondence for 1917, but of course our mother did *not* think it 'too dreadfully cool', because apparently the children's holidays were duly spent with us at a cost of £1 a week each, according to another extant letter from Mrs Blair the following year.

8

Nineteen Eighteen: The Pagan

AMONG THE ORIGINAL papers in the *Orwell Archive* at the London University Library is a poem called 'The Pagan': a rough copy, with bits crossed off and lines reversed and corrected. But I recognise it very well indeed and all its circumstances. It was the first more-or-less love poem I ever received, and since it was probably the first more-or-less love poem Eric ever wrote, that may be why he preserved it when so much else was lost.

My own fair copy, on pale blue notepaper in Eric's tidiest hand-writing, was enclosed with a letter he wrote me to the Oxford High School in the Autumn term of 1918. I kept it safely for years, in a favourite book – *My Two Kings* by Mrs Evan Nepean – which I thought a very good book indeed. It was about Charles II and Monmouth, with chapter headings of the author's poetry which very much appealed to me.

Almost exactly twenty-two years later, in October 1940, I was living at 111 Elm Park Mansions, Chelsea. I had been re-reading *My Two Kings*, and it was lying on my bedroom windowsill when a landmine, falling just opposite, destroyed the

book and Eric's poem with it. I have tried repeatedly and un-
successfully to replace *My Two Kings*, but the edition seems
to have vanished for ever. However, since there *is* a copy in
the *Orwell Archive*, and since it is one of Eric's earliest works
which has never been published before, we can retrieve the
poem :

> *THE PAGAN*
> *So here are you, and here am I,*
> *Where we may thank our gods to be;*
> *Above the earth, beneath the sky,*
> *Naked souls alive and free.*
> *The autumn wind goes rustling by*
> *And stirs the stubble at our feet;*
> *Out of the west it whispering blows,*
> *Stops to caress and onward goes,*
> *Bringing its earthy odours sweet.*
> *See with what pride the setting sun*
> *Kinglike in gold and purple dies,*
> *And like a robe of rainbow spun*
> *Tinges the earth with shades divine.*
> *That mystic light is in your eyes*
> *And ever in your heart will shine.*

When I wrote back I suggested it should have been *unarmoured*
souls, not *naked* souls – it was our minds, our hopes, our
dreams, that were confided so freely and so guilelessly : we were
not cavorting around in the altogether. And I would have
preferred *veil* to *robe* which is too man-made for a natural
phenomenon. He agreed with these amendments, and later
wrote them into my copy – with the original two words
crossed out. He said that would make it 'more authentic' than
re-writing the whole poem : more like 'more trouble-saving'.
And he also played with the idea of contracting it into a son-

net – but I liked all the nine first lines and we could not decide
which to leave out – and re-arranging the last six to run more
conventionally ABC ABC instead of ABA CBC. But I liked it
as it was, and am glad that I told him so.

At the time that we saw that sunset, we both said we would
never forget it. And I never have. Whenever there is a particularly beautiful sky, I am reminded of that golden evening, so
long ago when we were young.

I thought of it again last year, near Midsummer, when Guiny
and I had not decided what to call our new home. This is the
last house on a corner, with the sea to the south and fields with
trees to the west: and as I was walking up the road towards
it, the sky behind was so lovely that I remembered once more
Eric's sunset, and in remembrance sang a little song:

> *Circle as the dance*
> *Begins*
> *By the sun or Widdershins:*
> *Take your chance*
> *Till dance be done*
> *Widdershins or Way of Sun.*
>
> *All the seven*
> *Mortal sins*
> *Follow dancing Widdershins:*
> *But Heaven*
> *Sets a jewelled crown*
> *On Sun Dance as the sun goes down.*

It is not until the end of the dance that we realise the inevitable
consequences: the Breughel terrors following *Widdershins*,
and the golden glory crowning the *Circuit of the Sun*. But it is
by the innocent at the beginning that the choice must be made,
unknowing, for good or ill. It's a bit of magic for Midsummer's

Eve, or a children's game, like Oranges and Lemons, or a philosophy of life, or what you will. There is no name for the song, but from it the name of the house became Sun Dance.

*   *   *   *

We had been picking mushrooms in the fields beside the Harpsden woods. And in the highest field, resting on the thyme-sweet turf, with the basket between us, we talked and talked as the sun went down on that September evening in 1918.

It must have been the earlier part of September, because it was shortly before Auntie Lilian's wedding: my bridesmaid's-present brooch is engraved Sept 18th 1918. We remember the bad as well as the good, and one of the embarrassingly bad is *bricks we have dropped*. Auntie Lilian was not in her first youth when she married at thirty-nine, but her husband-to-be was over sixty. I had declaimed at some length on how incomprehensible it was that she could contemplate matrimony with a man old enough to be her father – when I suddenly realised that that was exactly the situation between Mr and Mrs Blair. Whether Eric took so much for granted the discrepancy between his parents' ages that he did not even notice this *faux pas*, or whether I passed it off successfully with a rather lame last-minute edict that *some* people were different, I have no idea. The subject was swiftly discarded.

Most of our conversation was about Oxford, and the wonderful time we should have when we got there. We reckoned that it would be quite feasible for us to be there together: I had started at boarding-school so late that I had had a good bit to catch up with – the French governesses had taught colloquial French, but the English ones only taught English. So Maths, Latin, and Greek were closed books to me. I adored Maths and got through all the missing back-work in my first term, but Latin was very heavy weather. The school's verdict was that I was so bad at it that it wasn't worth even trying me with Greek. This was disconcerting as I *wanted* to learn Greek.

RAB had taught me the Greek Alphabet very shortly after Grannifather Finlay taught me the English one: but though I can still recite *alphabetagammadelta* rapidly to the end, the rest of the Greek language is indeed Greek to me. Anyway, I reckoned I would be a year late getting to the University.

Eric, on the other hand, was an intelligent boy who had already proved himself capable of taking scholarships in his stride, and we had no doubt whatever that if he *worked* he would be equally successful with one of the Oxford Colleges. Once he was safely installed at Eton he had rather given up working: he said he deserved a rest after the intensive effort at St Cyprian's. But he was more than willing to re-apply himself to his studies given an incentive, and intended to start a campaign for parental permission. I had fired him with my own enthusiasm for Oxford. RAB had told me many inspiring stories of his sojourn there, and I thought it a glorious place – with the Bodleian and the Ashmolean and the Radcliffe Camera and what-not, even if it did not have *all* the facilities that I originally innocently imagined.

I had got into most frightful trouble in my first term at the Oxford High School. My parents were agnostics, because in their young day, with Darwin and his highly-publicised monkeys, that was the latest thing to be. But at the same time they had recounted to me the legends of almost every possible mythology: with the result that I was a natural Pantheist, believing implicitly and impartially in *all* the Gods.

For the first three weeks of term we girls were sent each Sunday to the nearest church. The fourth Sunday, on being told that the crocodile was set for the same destination, I refused to join it.

'But you *must* go to Church', said the Housemistress.

'Why?' I asked.

'To worship God, of course.'

'But that's only the Christian God', I argued, 'and we've

worshipped him three weeks running already. It's the turn for one of the others. Surely in a place the size of Oxford there must be a Temple of Astarte or somewhere we could go for a change?'

Angry as Miss Crosse was, thinking I was 'taking the Mickey' out of her, it was as nothing to her pained horror when she found I quite innocently *meant* it. And I was threatened to be removed from my dormitory and put in quarantine by myself if I did not mend such wicked ways – as well as having to report to the Headmistress on Monday morning. Luckily Miss Haig Brown was broader-minded, and I was let off with a lecture on current versus comparative religions. But I got my mother to write and insist that henceforth I should go to the Cathedral on Sundays – a sixth-form privilege which Miss Crosse was not at all pleased to accord to a lowly member of the fifth: but I thought if we were confined to the Christian God we might as well worship him in the best place.

I told this story to Eric that evening, which is why he called his poem *The Pagan*. And I remember we compared notes, too, about games. I had got my mother to *veto* games for me – that uncivilised unfeminine Hockey, and that silly Lacrosse – *never* would I be involved with such *barbarism*. So I had very special permission to go for instructive expeditions instead, which was why I was so up in the interesting exhibits of the vicinity. Eric envied me this permission to a certain degree but said that such a course would be impossible for *him*: public opinion would condemn it as unsporting, even if his father had been willing to play, which Eric even without asking knew he wouldn't. But I was a thoroughly unsporting type, dismissing the public opinion of misguided girls *willing* to play Hockey as simply not worth having. Eric steered a middle course over games: while he was not as devoted to them as the gregarious Prosper, he did not take the anathamatic view that I did

But there was no middle-course or compromise in his quiet

but absolute determination on his own ultimate career. It was always 'When I am a *FAMOUS AUTHOR* . . .', echoed by me 'Of course, when you are a *FAMOUS AUTHOR* . . .' This was another subject under discussion that September evening, and I think – though it *might* have been another time, it was always a popular subject with us – it was then that we decided on the format for his *Collected Works*. It was to be a Uniform Edition, and we argued at length on the respective merits of rather small books bound in red leather with gold lettering like my family's Kiplings, or somewhat larger in a chaste dark blue with silver, to which Eric was finally more inclined. RAB, when he was engaged and first married to my mother, had some books specially bound for her in dark green leather with gold fleur-de-lis as embellishment and gilt edges to the pages. I thought it would be rather nice for Eric to have a special De Luxe Set, after this pattern, but he, more Spartan, thought that might be 'a bit ostentatious'. In any case, he said, he wouldn't be writing that sort of book : but what was suitable for Darwin's *Origin of Species*, according to R A Buddicom, should have been appropriate to *E A Blair* whatever the subject matter. In those days he was going to be *E A Blair* – Eric, he said, was not an 'author's name': the initials were more dignified and could keep people guessing. I pointed out that far from assuming a staid and respectable *Edward*, people might guess it to stand for *Epimanondas* or something unprintable. And we had a lot of fun comparing the most frightful names beginning with E that we could think of.

It was not until sixteen years later that he adopted *George Orwell* as a rather spur-of-the-moment, last-minute decision. But the *FAMOUS AUTHOR*, with the collected editions, by the magic of that far-off sun-enchanted evening, was a dream that came true. Though Eric, alas, only lived to see the beginning of it.

But our united dreams of sharing the delights of Oxford

together were lost in the mists of that river city. Eric's father was adamant that his son should follow the parental footsteps to the Indian Civil. And my family decreed that such funds as were available should be concentrated on sending Prosper to Harrow and Brasenose, and that any further education was both impracticable and unnecessary for me. RAB had been a scientist, and a good one. So it was a pity that he fancied himself alternatively as *Big Business*, in several sidecat schemes. The family finances had suffered severely from hauling him out of the various holes into which he had so lightly leapt without looking, and the hitherto solvent Ticklerton was heavily mortgaged on his behalf before he shrugged everything off to try pioneering in Australia.

Poor, hopeful children that we were. I wonder what would have happened to our lives if we had been allowed to do what we quite reasonably wanted. In 1974, one does one's own thing. University Grants are to be had for the asking, and can be used by a hardcore to stage strikes, protest marches, and sit-ins, support unmarried bliss *ad lib* and to secure freedom from any sort of *work*, not caring that by their presence they are keeping out others who might make better use of their opportunities. But fifty or sixty years ago one did as one's parents ordained, and a University education had to be paid for. Even entering for a scholarship required parental consent: and if that consent were not forthcoming, there was no more to be said or done.

* * * *

At some time during 1918 Mrs Blair had removed from her room in Earls Court and taken an extremely small flat in Notting Hill Gate – 23 Mall Chambers. This was never a 'family home', it was simply a *pied-à-terre* from which Mrs Blair could conveniently work in London, and the real family home at 36 St Marks Road was not given up. It was let furnished on a series of short tenancies, and as far as I can remember was retained for the Blairs' own use at times during the children's Easter and/or Summer holidays, when Mrs Blair took some leave.

In November 1918 she wrote to our mother :

23 Mall Chambers
The Mall
Notting Hill Gate
W.8.
5.11.18

My dear Mrs Buddicom

I really feel half nervous of trying to make plans ahead, but *if* all goes well with our respective families, do you think you could have Eric and Avril for the Xmas holidays, they have implored me to ask you & I promised I would, but I shall *quite* understand if you don't feel equal to undertaking it, but if you do, perhaps you would let me know what you could take them for, things have risen so in price that I know you could not possibly have them for £1 a week which is what you suggested last year, anyway let me know & then I can write to my husband about it. Avril is just getting over flu, the second attack she has had this year. I am thankful to say she is now on the mend but has been in bed nearly 3 weeks with it : they are most careful at her school & she is getting all the care she needs I know. I go down on Saturday afternoons & sit with her, it is about my only available time. I had Marge home last week on a few days leave. She is now a despatch rider for the Women's Legion & is stationed at Warminster. She loves her work & is looking so much better for being in the open air.

I hope you & yours are all well.

Yours very sincerely
Ida Blair

Evidently following on this comes another letter, undated :

23 Mall Chambers
Notting Hill Gate W.8.

My dear Mrs. Buddicom

I have today heard from my husband who is quite willing for Eric & Avril to go to you for the holidays for the sum you

78

mentioned in your letter of Nov. 6 i.e. £4.0.0. a week. Avril I know breaks up on Tuesday Dec. 17th, but I am not yet certain about Eric. I hope to go to Eton next Sat. for his confirmation & will then find out for certain the day his holidays begin & will let you know. Avril is now all right, but she will not be able to bicycle in the holidays or do anything strenuous. However as it is the winter there will not be so much temptation for her to want to 'gallivant'! It is very kind of you to undertake the care of them & I hope nothing will occur between now & the holidays to prevent their going to you.

Yours very sincerely
Ida Blair

There are more letters regarding the 1918 Christmas:

23 Mall Chambers
The Mall
Notting Hill Gate W.8.
13.12.18

My dear Mrs. Buddicom

I ought to have written yesterday to acknowledge your letter & the £1.0.0. which I got quite safely on Wednesday evening – I got a letter from Prosper a few days ago telling me what time he hopes to reach town. Now about my chicks. It seems *Eric* breaks up on 17th & Avril 18th. I don't know what train Eric will go by, he usually leaves at some very early hour, but I'll tell him to try & arrange for a later train as I don't want him to pounce on you too early! I will let you know later what time Avril will be arriving on Wed. 18th. She has not been allowed to do anything strenuous yet & of course no bicycling these holidays must she do. I am afraid she will be disappointed but it can't be helped. I hope to go down to her school tomorrow & will then send you a p.c. to tell you her train.

Yours very sincerely
Ida Blair

P.S.

I see I have never said anything about Boxing Day which you so kindly invited us down for. I am afraid I can't accept as we are to go to my sisters for that Day. It is so kind of you to have asked us – Ida Blair

79

23 Mall Chambers
Notting Hill Gate W.8.
21.12.18

My dear Mrs. Buddicom

I sent off a parcel directed to you yesterday with some Xmas presents which please give to the children on Xmas morning. Avril always has a stocking so I put in a few odds & ends for it which will you please put in a stocking for her on Xmas Eve night. I enclose £9.15 in this – £8.0.0 for you please for 2 weeks for the children & will you please give Eric 25/- from his Father & 6/- from his Aunt Nellie & Avril 4/- from her Aunt Nellie. I am so sorry I can't manage to come down for Xmas, but I have Marjorie here & one of my sisters is coming to me on Xmas Day. I am hoping to be able to run down one Sat. before the holidays end. I had a letter from the head mistress of Avril's school telling me again how careful Avril must be these holidays. If she wants to go into Henley at all will you please tell her she must go by train. She has only been going a short walk every day & been leading an absolutely quiet life. I feel sure you will see she does nothing at all strenuous, but as I had that letter I thought I would just mention the subject again as she can't be too careful.

I shall think of you all at Xmas time & I need not wish you a happy time as I am sure you will all be most happy together. I am so grateful to you for having the chicks & so glad to think they are with you. With all good wishes

Yours very sincerely
Ida Blair

So the Blairs spent the Christmas holidays with us at Quarry House. There is mention of this in a couple of letters from Nors, at the time stationed at Ipswich (where he waited long and patiently to be demobilised). On 23rd December he writes to our mother: 'I hope the Xmas Tree party will go off all right & that you will not tire yourself out with all the children.' And on 28th December: 'Please thank the kids for their letters, it was good of them to write again as the 2 girls had already thanked me. They seem to have done rather well in the money line this Christmas . . . I hope you are feeling more cheerful & not so depressed. You ought to feel quite happy with all those kids roaming round you.'

Our mother had a good many 'kids roaming round her' during those holidays, as after Christmas there were more juvenile visitors: my schoolfriend Norma Lewis, still my friend under different names: after being widowed as Mrs John Hodgson she is now Mrs Alexander Russell. And the daughter of RAB's friend and fellow-lecturer, G P Mudge, Phyllis, who was about the same age. And a schoolfriend of Prosper's, Cedric Goldie. It was a bit of a problem to find space for so many: I think two of the boys had to share a room and someone had to sleep on the nursery sofa. But we all had a very happy time, with the war over and no fear of any *more* friends and relations being killed. Phyllis had lost her only brother, Aubrey, aged just nineteen. But Norma's brother Maurice was safe.

9

Nineteen Nineteen:
After the War

EARLY IN JANUARY Prosper, Guiny, and Eric all went back with Cedric Goldie to stay with his family in Bournemouth. He must have been a good-hearted and generous boy, because almost as soon as they had arrived he sent me the biggest box of the most magnificent chocolates I had ever seen in my life, as a consolation present for not being able to accompany them.

On the journey from Shiplake to Bournemouth they had to change at Basingstoke with an hour's wait between trains. There was a canal nearby, so Eric suggested fishing in it with a bent pin (to be supplied by Guiny, but if not already bent he would kindly bend it) and a bit of string. No reasonable opportunity for fishing ever escaped him – or unreasonable, for that matter, since the Basingstoke canal was hardly a likely habitation for fish.

There was a poster to be seen on railway stations around that time, or a little later, which took our fancy. It was illustrated by a fat cat and a skeleton cat, with the catchy rhyme:

The ghost of Tabby fed on skim
Is all the war has left of him:
But Thomas is a well-fed cat
With NESTLE'S CREAM full to the brim.

If anyone has a copy left, I should like it now. Basingstoke, incidentally, was Eric's best 'buried town':

THE QUEEN OF SHEBA SINGS TO KEEP HER SPIRITS UP.

There is a letter to our mother from Guiny on this visit:

> Osborne Grange
> Branksome Park
> Bournemouth
> Jan. 8th 1919

Dear Mits

I hope Avril is looking after the animals all right. I hope she is. You had better remind her some times to feed them as she may forget and they would die. Tell her not to forget to cover the rabbits every Night, for if they are left they will catch cold if the night is cold. If Nitce is at home he might help her. Tell her not to forget Josphs ear, to be done every other day.

I have got a comb in Bournemouth. Tell Cini I have finished 2 books already and nearly finished a third.

Why don't you write? ...

> Very much love
> to her Mother
> From her
> Apy.

It was to Avril that the care of the animals was delegated, despite the fact that I was on the premises. My interest was confined to cats – my school letters are full of references and messages to 'my *own* cat' – Quillie – and I was never involved with any of the minor livestock to which the others were so attached, and for which it was mostly Guiny who had the care with Prosper away at school. At that time she was eleven and Avril ten: they were both capable and trustworthy children, so I am sure that Guiny's precious rabbits were safe with Avril.

The three returned from that visit full of enthusiasm for the splendour of the Goldies' household and the grandeur of their food. That family was obviously much richer than we were. They returned, also, singing ceaselessly a song that had been taught to them by Cedric Goldie's little sister. She must have been a *very* little sister, because they sang it in the same way that she did :

> Sir Wodger is dead an' he lies in his g'ave,
> Heigh, Ho, Lies in his G'ave . . .

Eric certainly never gave any indication of being poverty-conscious on this occasion. He seemed quite as appreciative of the comparative luxury as Prosper and Guiny, but no more abashed than they were at its being beyond our common scope.

It was during these Christmas holidays that Eric wrote me another poem. He produced various poems on various occasions, and when he was at Eton and I was at the Oxford High School, we wrote to each other nearly every week.

We always began our letters to each other, 'Hail and Fare Well', in two separate words because we were already apart and wished each other Good Fortune, ending 'Farewell and Hail', so that we should meet again. Eric's letters were very interesting : mostly long and literary reviews of whatever books he happened to be reading – with recommendation or otherwise – and general philosophy. There was never a word of *politics*. Whether or not he was as preoccupied with them as he is said to have been, he never in his schooldays discussed them either with me or with Prosper. But his letters – with or without poetry – were always full of entertainment and I had preserved them very carefully, in a white shoebox tied up with red string, which when we left Shiplake in 1921 I took up to Ticklerton for safe keeping. At Shiplake we were often moving from one house to another and treasures got stuck away at random into the *shed*, sometimes behind massive piles and unget-atable, so I thought Ticklerton would be more static and less violate.

When Malcolm Muggeridge advertised for Orwell information (some time in the late 1950s, I think) I rang him up and told him I had these documents: but he did not pursue the matter, so I concluded he was not interested. This was a pity, because they could certainly have been preserved then – Auntie Lilian was most meticulous about other peoples' property. But after she died in 1964, the family solicitor/trustee destroyed a mass of papers wholesale – my letters from Eric presumably among them. For when I read the catalogue of what were being put up for sale – things which, though of no vast value, had been in the family for a couple of hundred years – I rushed up to try to retrieve some, and Eric's letters were then nowhere to be found. It was all very unfortunate. And ironic that if I *had* left them in the Shiplake shed they would doubtless have been as well preserved as all the other odds and ends we unearthed there in 1969.

From the far-off days of over fifty years ago, a few special occasions stand out as clearly as the day before yesterday. One was the sunset evening just before Auntie Lilian's wedding: I promised at the time always to remember it, and so, since there have been many other lovely sunsets, it has been so frequently recalled as to be kept forever constant in my mind. Another such special occasion was during the houseparty of the 1918-19 Christmas holidays.

We were in the dining-room at Quarry House: the old nursery had been commandeered as a bedroom, so we played in the dining-room. Quarry House was a good example of the Art Nouveau of the early nineteen hundreds, so the drawing-room and dining-room were interestingly irregular, not just oblong boxes. The drawing-room had a four-sided bay, with sofas, in the south-west corner which got all the sun from morning till night, and french windows to a tiled inset-porch below the first-floor balcony, where we had tea in the summer. The window to the north of this porch was the same south window of the dining-room where the robin came for his breakfast butterpats. The dining-room also had a north glazed door to the garden – a useful means of escape when un-appreciated visitors were observed ringing the front doorbell – and a large west window from whence Prosper and Eric fired for target-practice to a point below the gravel-pit bank a measured hundred yards away. The lower half of the room was cased in panelling stained green, with the upper half plain tuck-pointed brick matched by the terra-cotta velour curtains. The furniture was of light oak, constructed to RAB's own design by a tame Socialist carpenter who was a friend of his, and the chairs had green leather seats to match the panelling.

On the north side of the room was a very large alcove, headed by a narrow panel below the ceiling, handpainted by some early Edwardian artist with a glade of bluebells, of which I was very fond, bluebells being my own name-flowers. The fireplace was in the middle of this alcove: on the west was a built-in writing-desk complete with pigeon-holes and window, on the east was an ingle-nook box-seat at right-angles to the fire. Altogether, in winter time, a very cosy corner indeed.

And this was winter, with a bright fire blazing but not yet late enough in the afternoon for the lamps to be lit. (No electricity at Quarry House in 1919, though Gran had it at Burwood by 1911.) Eric was sitting at the desk, presumed to be writing to his parents. I was curled up on cushions, Quillie curled up beside me, on the ingleseat with a book. The others were all at the large oblong dining-table, playing some card-game fairly quietly so as not to disturb us.

But Eric had not been occupied solely with family corres-pondence: he had, at intervals, been composing a sonnet for me. This, written on rough, lined paper from an old exercise book, he presented with some pomp and circumstance at the first opportunity of adequate privacy :

> Our minds are married, but we are too young
> For wedlock by the customs of this age
> When parent homes pen each in separate cage
> And only supper-earning songs are sung.
>
> Times past, when medieval woods were green,
> Babes were betrothed, and that betrothal brief.
> Remember Romeo in love and grief –
> Those star-crossed lovers – Juliet was fourteen.
>
> Times past, the caveman by his new-found fire
> Rested beside his mate in woodsmoke's scent.
> By our own fireside we shall rest content
> Fifty years hence keep troth with hearts desire.
>
> We shall remember, when our hair is white,
> These clouded days revealed in radiant light.

I always saw the cavemen as the picture at the beginning of the Kipling *History Book* – which may be where Eric got the idea from. I do remember those days now in radiant light : eternal echo of that firelit, winter afternoon.

But that was Eric's idea, which was unfortunately and re-grettably never mine. He was a perfect companion and I was very fond of him – as literary guide-philosopher-and-friend. But I had no romantic emotion for him. The two years be-tween a girl of seventeen and a boy of fifteen, as a beginning, are just the wrong two years. At fifteen, he was certainly too young to be married : but at seventeen I *might* have been mar-riageable to someone older.

*   *   *   *

87

When I was thirteen, I was not in love – since I was no Lolita – but in my childish fashion very much attached to Noel Wallis, a young bachelor solicitor, a friend of RAB's, who sometimes stayed at Quarry House. He was very nice indeed and treated children as reasonable people, which all our elders did *not*: you were mostly either talked down to, or heavy-handedly humoured.

I remember exactly the moment I became aware of him. There was a family house-party, probably in early April or May 1914 – it is a springtime atmosphere – and we had been having tea in the drawing-room. I think Prosper and Guiny had gone out to play in the garden, but I'd stayed on with the grown-ups.

Our mother, RAB, Nors, and Uncle Dudie were there: so was Auntie Mimi with her husband Noël Burke, and I was sitting on a tuffet beside Noel Wallis. The Burkes had been married for not much more than a year, and were full of en-thusiasm for their happy state. It was an ideal marriage, and lasted with unfailing love until Mrs Burke's death in 1960. Noël was broken-hearted, inconsolable till he followed her in 1964.

Auntie Mimi declared that Noel Wallis ought to get mar-ried: 'Noël's make splendid husbands'; but Noel Wallis just laughed, and ruffled my hair, and said, 'I'll wait for Jacintha.'

Of course that was purely the pleasantest pleasantry, a polite way of telling Mrs Burke to mind her own business: but when he said it, there was a lightning-flash of illumination to my mind that, some very long way ahead, in the very far distant future, when I was fearfully old – nineteen perhaps – it might not be at all a bad idea to be married to our nice Noel Wallis who was so kind to us all, and who had always made rather a special pet of me.

*   *   *   *

In January 1971, when I was sorting through the Shiplake

papers, to take some up to Ian Angus for the *Orwell Archive*, I found a newspaper cutting:

SECOND LIEUTENANT NOEL VEDER WALLIS, who was killed on April 10, was the third son of the late William Emerson Wallis, of Lloyd's, and Mrs Wallis of Wilmar, Broadstone, Dorset, and grandson of the late Mr James Seabrook, of Grays, Essex, and was 35 years of age. He was educated at Tonbridge and University College, Oxford, and was established as a solicitor in London. He left his business to join the Army, and after serving in Egypt and Salonika, whence he was sent home suffering from malaria, he rejoined; being posted to the Cheshire Regiment, and left for the front last February.

I hadn't cried since Paddy died in September 1960 – I never cry for people nowadays, only for cats. But I cried then most bitterly for Noel Wallis. Not just because he had been so very nice, and it was so sad for him to have been killed at only thirty-five. But because, fifty-five years later, until I discovered that cutting, I had forgotten all about him.

Many waters cannot quench love – except the waters of Lethe. Was it Mary Rose who showed us that people may be forgotten as time goes by?

> As time goes by do we forget?
> Do we forget – I don't know yet.
> I don't know yet – we don't know why –
> We don't know why. And time goes by.
>
> The time goes by and you are gone.
> And you are gone – my life goes on –
> My life goes on but where am I?
> But where am I, while time goes by.
>
> The time goes by through nights and days:
> Through nights and days, remembrance stays.
> While memory stays love does not die –
> Love does not die as time goes by.

Memory is the light that shines through the echoing limbo of the lost ones. But who is lost – the one who is gone, or the one who is left behind?

*   *   *   *

There is another letter written by Mrs Blair to our mother during the 1919 January holidays:

> 23 Mall Chambers
> Notting Hill Gate W.8.
> 15.1.19

Dear Mrs. Buddicom
  I am sorry to say I won't be able to have the children this week end after all, as I heard by the first post this morning that my husband is coming home on leave today, & as the flat is so tiny we could not possibly all squeeze in. [*So much for 'family home'.*] So will you keep the children till the end of the holidays. Avril has to be back at school on Tuesday 21st (afternoon) so will you tell her to inquire at Shiplake station about trains direct to Ealing. I wd like her to get there fairly early, about 2 or 3 if possible. I am so sorry Dick hasn't sent any further money for the chicks, but now he's coming home he will be able to settle it all up. I hope the delay hasn't inconvenienced you at all, can you tell me exactly what we owe you for now, as you gave Eric back the £2. I've lost count. I can't tell you how grateful I am for all you have done.
> Yours very sincerely
> Ida Blair

I suppose the *mystiquites* will want to quote *this* as evidence of the Blairs' dire poverty – quite forgetting the commonplace restrictions and difficulties caused by family separation at this period, with the War barely over and men still not knowing where they were going to be posted next.

  In a letter from Auntie Lilian to our mother dated 7 March 1919 she says:

> Will it suit you for Prosper and Guinever to come to us from 14th April to 24th? . . . Prosper asked to bring Eric & provided

we have servants which we quite hope, we shall be very pleased to see him – the children I shall manage anyhow.

But she writes again on March 10th :

> I think I had better *not* ask Eric . . . I am afraid that even if we have a house parlourmaid *three* young people would be too much for Mrs Butler. She is an *excellent* cook & most respectable & it would be a great thing if she wd stay through the summer as I could leave her in charge if John and I go away – but she is oh! so difficile! Always ready to take offence! Always just going to give notice! And I daren't risk offending her!! She never leaves the kitchen, so that one other servant is not really enough to keep the house even decent, as Father & John both need a lot of attending on, & we have late dinner. She doesn't even sweep the back passages in the morning! – All the same, she is a great comfort in the house & *such* a good cook. We look forward so much to seeing Prosper and Guinever on the 14th. I don't feel we can get in a visit from Jacintha in the Easter holidays. Anyway if she waits till August we should hope for a long visit & the fares are still so expensive that it would be better if she were to come for one long visit than two short ones. When you next write to Prosper will you kindly tell him that *at present* we don't see our way to invite Eric on account of domestic difficulties. I daren't risk losing Mrs Butler. I do hope Prosper will pass into Harrow all right.

There is a letter from Prosper complaining of this change of plan.

Writing to our mother from Ticklerton on April 18th 1919, Guiny asks: 'Has Queen had her kittens yet?' The others all called her Queen: it was only I who called her Quillie, my special name for my special cat.

There is a letter I wrote to Guiny from the High School Boarders house :

St Frideswides
Bardwell Road
Oxford
June 1st 1919

Dearest Apy

Many thanks for your letter. If you want to give me a book, I should like one about Dr Nikola – the only one we have is 'Dr Nikola' – there are others, 'Dr Nikola's Experiment', 'A Bid for Fortune', 'Farewell Nikola'. You could get one of these – in a cheap edition, do not go spending a lot of money – but if you are hard up, do not bother to get me anything. It is very kind of you to think of it all the same. [*All these had been recommended by Eric.*]

There is no news. My love to Mits. She has not answered my letter yet.

I am looking forward to coming home on the 20th. There were 'Eights' on all last week. The way they work is like this: in each race (there are 3 each day for 4 days) there are eight or nine boats of eight men each. They do not all start off together, but one at a time after short intervals. Each boat tries to catch up with the boat in front and 'bump' it – (i.e. bash into it.) It is very exciting, but nothing like the Henley Regatta. The undergrads rush along the towpath after the boats, yelling and shrieking and blowing whistles and letting off pistols. I daresay you would like it.

Love from
Cini

How is my own cat? Are her kittens sold yet?

I came home for half-term on June 20th. It was that forever frozen sunny summer day when Quillie was not there.

*   *   *   *

The end of the term was the end of my education: so it was a good thing the philosophical Eric was around in the summer holidays to give me sympathetic encouragement. He was not there all the time, because the Blairs went for a holiday to Cornwall – Polperro, I think – and Prosper accompanied them. They had had Cornish holidays in previous years, and from one of these Eric brought back a couple of anecdotes which he

92

regaled to us with gusto. We always swapped any 'funny stories' we heard or read, and Eric's sometimes had a rather macabre flavour, as witness these Cornish ones.

The first we heard repeated on television, only the other day. Tradition lingers long: I don't suppose it was *new* fifty years and more ago, when Eric recounted it in a smock-and-forelock accent:

'Marnin, Jarge.'

'Marnin, John.'

'Wot yew give yewr old oss wen e ad the bloind staggers?'

'Turr-pentoine, turr-pentoine.'

'Zo did oi, but moine doid!'

'Zo did moine! Zo did moine!'

The second was the straightforward tale of a husband and wife who went on holiday to Cornwall. The husband went out sea-fishing, when his boat overturned and he fell into the water and disappeared. The wife waited a few days but there was no sign of him, so she returned home, leaving her address for immediate news. Next day she received a telegram: 'Your husband washed up on beach. Body covered with crabs. What shall we do?' To which she replied: 'Sell the crabs for as much as you can and re-set the bait.'

Guiny did not think much of this latter story, saying it was a crib on the *Ingoldsby Legends*:

> *Go – pop Sir Thomas again in the Pond*
> *Poor dear! – he'll catch us some more!!*

My own favourite anecdote of the period, from the comic pages of *Pearson's Magazine*, or some such periodical, and which Eric appreciated equally, showed a stolid-looking policeman with a walrus moustache, on guard outside a Bank: with a very young and excited reporter rushing up to him:

REPORTER: I'm from the Daily Wail, come to do the robbery.

CONSTABLE: You're too late, my lad – the robbery's been done.

Eric gives honourable mention to *The Ingoldsby Legends* in the *Collected Essays*, Vol 3, p 328, crediting Barham with 'a feat of sheer virtuosity which the most serious poet would respect', and saying: 'Early Victorian light verse is generally haunted by the ghost of poetry; it is often extremely skilful as verse, and it is sometimes allusive and "difficult".' (*Leader*, 28 July 1945). But although on the same page he quotes Belloc with due regard (I well remember his penchant for the quoted 'O Africa') he is not so kind to others:

> English light verse in the present century – witness the work of Owen Seaman, Harry Graham, A. P. Herbert, A. A. Milne, and others – has mostly been poor stuff, lacking not only in fancifulness but intellectuality. Its authors are too anxious not to be highbrows – even, though they are writing in verse, not to be poets.

A harsh and very 1944 judgment. As a boy he was particularly fond of the frivolities of Harry Graham, which he quoted by the mile. For example, from the verses entitled 'Exaggeration':

> *How people do exaggerate!*
> *One fable soon begets another.*
> *For instance, I have heard folks state*
> *That they have seen me throw a plate,*
> *Two dumb-bells and a paperweight*
> *At Mother.*
> *The story is of course untrue –*
> *It was the teapot that I threw.*

or the equally enjoyed 'Presence of Mind':

> *If your bulldog lay hold of a stranger*
> *You should turn the thing off with a laugh,*
> *Saying, 'Nonsense! Your leg's in no danger –*
> *My bull is quite cowed by your calf!'*
> *If the stranger reply to you thickly*

> *Or to water be vainly decoyed,*
> *Then both he and the dog should be quickly*
> *Destroyed.*

Herbert and Milne were not yet writing when we were young, but I think have produced various gems far above Harry Graham. And Eric was not always poetically serious in 1919.

*   *   *   *

Nors had been demobilised, and so had Uncle Dudie, now living at Phyllis Court and with a small motor-launch. Prosper and I spent a fair amount of time with him, and it was quite fun being grown-up – though 'up' was not very far as I only achieved a height of five feet and half-an-inch, a weight of 6 stone 2 lb, (86 pounds in America) and very Vital Statistics of 32-21-31.

Although Uncle Dudie kept open house at Phyllis', I think Eric only went there once, and then didn't seem to enjoy it much. The next time we suggested he should meet us there, he said he hated crowds and complained that there were too many people.

Of course there always *were* a lot of people. After all, it was a *club*, and many friends of the members as well as Uncle Dudie's, were demobilised now and glad to rest by the tranquil river after the turmoil of war. So there were plenty of parties. I remember one rather Alice-like afternoon being taken to Temple Island in a punt, by a visiting Australian. He was tall and fair with a moustache, and his name was Fred Salusbury. He, too, was going to write, and he recited me some of his poetry. When we got back to Phyllis – late for tea – he wrote it down on Phyllis Court paper. I never met him again after that visit, but I remember the poems in part, though the manuscript, signed unforgettably FGHS, was lost long ago, like so much else. One I can recall completely :

95

The old grey rocks stand side by side
Their beards afloat on the swaying tide
That reaches a seemingly timid hand
And grasps at the stretch of shining sand
Leaving a sky-swept stain:
The water's green and the water's cool,
The sea swings into each restless pool,
And hastens out again.

I liked the poems, because they were short and vivid pictures; but there remain only the first two verses of another one:

Rouen with roofs a-glisten
Lies calm beneath the moon:
It's a night on which to listen
To a half-forgotten tune,
To the lilt of long-dead laughter
And the tap of buckled shoon.

The scent of climbing roses
Hangs heavy on the air:
A gate ajar discloses
A winding, grey stone stair,
And a hooded form descending
With a glint of errant hair.

I wish I could remember the rest of it: it is an enchantment of ghosts. I always saw the roses as yellow like the moonlight: I don't know what colour they really were.

Mr Blair, also, was demobilised in 1919 and went back to his secretaryship at the Golf Club. The family were mostly living at 36 St. Marks Road again, but the *pied-à-terre* at 23 Mall Chambers was retained, I think to be occupied mainly by Marjorie and/or Mrs Blair's sister, working in London. I'm not sure exactly when Mrs Blair gave up her own war job, but she was certainly keeping an eye on the household during the children's school holidays. She may have partly commuted for a bit, or spent the midweek in London during termtime. Mr Blair, on his own, could always eat at the Golf Club.

For Christmas 1919 Eric gave me *Dracula*, which he had just discovered with great excitement. He was a particularly thoughtful and considerate boy, so, carefully wrapped in tissue-paper and packed separately, in the same parcel were a crucifix (he knew I would not be likely to have one) and a clove of garlic, difficult to obtain in Henley. These proven safeguards against vampires were to reassure me, so that I should have the pleasure of the book without being so scared by it as he had been. On the several occasions when I went to tea with him in St Marks Road that December and January, Eric escorted me all the way home although we went by train, so I should not have to walk up the long dark lane from Shiplake Station to Quarry House alone, with every bush a bear and the Count hanging batlike from any passing tree.

Prosper, that Christmas, had acquired *The School Boy's Pocket Diary and Notebook for* 1920 (Letts, 5¾" x 3½") with columns for pocket-money, marks, shooting-scores, books read, autographs, etc : and numerous pages of printed information, besides illustrations appended for every Saturday and nature-notes. But for some extraordinary reason the *endpapers* depict a moonlight glade peopled by fairies, elves, teddy-bears, rabbits, and toadstools: which any 1920 schoolboy would have scorned as cissy in the extreme.

On the *Books Read* page, Prosper has headed the column with *Robbery under Arms*, one of his own 1919 Christmas presents. And second on the list comes *Dracula*, evidently borrowed from me as soon as I had finished reading it myself.

Nineteen Twenty:
Prosper's Diary

PROSPER KEPT UP his 1920 diary most meticulously, with an entry for every day and column, so it is a goldmine of contemporary record for what was happening to us all, that year.

He starts on the *Memoranda* first page:

> Left Charing Cross for Switzerland on Monday Dec 19th 1919. Left Murren for England Jan 12th 1920.

And on Wednesday, 14 January he records:

> Came to Shiplake by 2.15 from Paddington. Found Guinever in bed. Jacintha had gone to Ticklerton on Monday.

So my recollection that Eric and I were very much on our own at that time is corroborated. Prosper had been taken for a Winter Sports holiday by Uncle Dudie – always a kind and generous Uncle – and Guiny had been suffering from the constantly recurring sub-acute rheumatism (diagnosed erroneously as 'just flu') which had affected her heart and which inflicted her with several long stays in bed. It must have been very dull and lonely for her, poor child, as all excitement was forbidden:

so Eric and I were discouraged from spending much time with her, although we ourselves met constantly during these holidays.

He often bicycled over to Shiplake, and I went to tea with him in St Marks Road more frequently than before. But of course we were older. Two teenagers talking quietly about literature would be less obstreperous than five younger children playing noisy games. Even a comparatively peaceful game with five children can be pandemonium.

Prosper notes for Friday, 16 January:

> Jacintha came home from Ticklerton. Uncle Dudie came over for lunch. Started packing to go to Ticklerton tomorrow.

My visit to Ticklerton had been very brief: only to 'come out' at the Shrewsbury Hunt Ball. Prosper, accompanied by Guiny, who by then was obviously better, went up for the shooting from 17 to 24 January. Of the 23rd he says:

> Went out shooting in Edge Wood with Ted and Uncle John. Guin shot 5 rabbits and 1 pheasant, and I shot 2 rabbits. We got in all 10 rabbits and 2 pheasants.

Guiny was a good shot. It was very creditable for her to have got half the bag herself, aged as yet not quite thirteen.

On 28 January Prosper notes that he went back to Harrow. It seems rather late in the month for the beginning of term? There is no mention of Eric in Prosper's diary for the three clear days he was at home before returning to school, so presumably Eric was not in Henley then. The Eton term might have started earlier, or Eric might have been at Mall Chambers, or elsewhere.

On Easter Monday, 5 April, the holidays start:

> Came home from Harrow by the 9 o'clock from Paddington. Found Guin in bed. Had 9 eggs from the hens. Best we have had.

After this, through the rest of the holidays, Eric appears almost every day all through April:

7 Wednesday   Eric came over in morning and brought a .22 rifle. We went out shooting & got 3 birds.

8 Thursday   Went to Reading with the Blairs to the Cinema. Bought 50 .410 cartridges size 2½". Also bought a ramrod for .22 rifle.

9 Friday   Eric came over in morning and we went out shooting. Only got a starling. Went in to Henley in afternoon and bought some cartridges.

10 Saturday   Eric came over in morning. Had target practice with .22 rifle. I got 42 and 47 out of 50. Guin got 39 out of 50. [*No mention of what Eric got: perhaps he was not shooting with them, but talking to me? J.B.*]

11 Sunday   Jacintha and I went in to lunch & tea at the Club [Phyllis] with Uncle Dudie. Mits went to tea with the Burkes.

12 Monday   Found some .22 long cartridges & had target practice. Got 78 out of 100, 106 out of 150 at decimal [?] target & 48 out of 50 at ordinary target.

13 Tuesday   Went out shooting in morning with Eric. He got 5 birds & I got 2. Went in to tea in afternoon to Henley with Eric & Avril. Bought 200 cart.

14 Wednesday   Eric came over in morn & afternoon & had tea. Went out shooting & shot 2 birds.

15 Thursday   Had lunch and tea at the Golf Club with Eric. Went out shooting & shot 4 birds & a squirrel. Played Koun Kan & Eucre in evening.

16 Friday   I shot a pigeon in morning. Eric came over in afternoon & had tea. We went out shooting with rifles & got 2 birds.

17 Saturday   Eric came over in morning & afternoon. He shot a partridge [Out of season?*! *Wretched young savages, shooting all these birds – mostly just* garden *birds in the nesting season. J.B.*] We went out birds' nesting but only found one or two nests.

18 Sunday   Eric came over in morning & had tea with us in afternoon. Nephew of Holloway came up. [*The Holloways were friends in Shiplake. J.B.*]

19 Monday   Went to Henley to see Uncle Dudie but as he had visitors did not go. Went to lunch with Eric instead. Went out shooting.

20 Tuesday   Went into Henley to see Uncle Dudie & had lunch there. Also stayed the night to see him off to Cambridge tomorrow. [*He went to Trinity Hall as an ex-army student. J.B.*]

21 Wednesday   Had breakfast at Phyllis & came home afterwards. Eric came to lunch and tea. Shot 5 birds.

22 Thursday   Went into Reading & to the cinema with Eric & Jacintha. Shot a partridge. Bought some patience cards.

23 Friday   Eric & Mrs. Blair came to tea in afternoon. Got 10 eggs from hens, the first time this year. Played Roulette etc :

24 Saturday   Eric came over in morning & we played Roulette. I lost 11d.

25 Sunday   Eric came over to tea. We made some bombs which exploded by Sulph Acid on sugar & KCl.

26 Monday   Went over to lunch & tea with Eric at Golf Club. I hit cuckoo but it got away.

27 Tuesday   Eric came over to lunch & tea. We played Roulette & cards. I won 4d. & Guin 9d.

28 Wednesday   Eric came over in afternoon. Played Roulette. I won 1/5 & Jacintha won 1/2½d. [*We played with farthings, of which we had a large collection, and cashed up at the end of the game. J.B.*]

29 Thursday   Went over to Golf Club to lunch with Eric in morning & he came back with me in afternoon.

30 Friday   Started for school by 1.12 from Shiplake. Came up with Eric & Jacintha. Went to cinema in town.

This diary is of no particular moment as *Great Literature*, but it gives a useful contemporary record of the typical frequency with which we saw Eric when we were all living at Shiplake and Henley. Of the twenty-six days, including arrival and departure, of those Easter holidays, Eric was with us on twenty-one. Of course, Prosper notes the advent of Eric so unfailingly because he was not living in the house with us : the presence of Guiny and me is usually taken for granted. Avril might not always be mentioned if she were only playing with Guiny, but she might not have been there all the time. Mrs Blair is only mentioned once, as coming to tea on a Friday afternoon, and the fact that Prosper on three occasions notes that he had lunch with Eric at the Golf Club looks rather as though at that time she was probably commuting : otherwise they would have more likely had lunch at St Marks Road if she had been at home. None of us seem to have gone to Ticklerton during those holidays, nor did Prosper's schoolfriends come to stay. But a letter from Grandpapa Buddicom to me dated 16 April refers to Quarry House being let, and the envelope is addressed to The Shanty, where there was far less accommodation.

There is a letter to our mother from Eric, that summer term. The envelope is lost, but the letter is written on large-sized pad-paper, not folded notepaper, watermarked 'SOCIETY BOND cream wove J.W. & CO. LTD.' – though, perhaps with age, it looks more like a grubby grey – and with printed heading :

ETON COLLEGE
WINDSOR
27/6/20

My dear Mrs. Buddicome

You said very kindly last holidays that I might come & watch the race at Henley on the 30th from your punt. Do you still intend going there, & may I come? I should be very glad if you could let me know before Wednesday. I am sorry I have given you such short notice; if you are not going I shall of course spend the day with my Father. I shall be very glad if you could tell me your arrangements & where & when to meet you. I might pick you up at Shiplake, as my train would pass there about 11.35 or so. I am going to meet my Father in Henley.

I hope the weather will be a little better than it is today on Wednesday.

Yours sincerely
Eric Blair.

At the end of this letter are two sketches of him : one in pencil by himself, a very pear-shaped caricature, the other a pen copy by me, much more like him. He does not mention his mother, so she must have been in London : but note that his first choice is to spend his exeat with the Buddicom Family, his father – whom he nevertheless intended to meet – taking second place.

Eton, as a rowing school, always sent an Eight to the Henley Regatta, for which the boys had a holiday on the first day, the Wednesday. If they got through to the Final, they had a further holiday to see it on the Saturday. Harrow – on the Hill, with no river – had no Eight, nor any Regatta Exeat either.

Prosper, at this time, had measles : his entry for 30 June, that Regatta Wednesday, reads :

> Speech Day. Still in bed in sick room. Hollingsworth (his Housemaster) sent up an ice.

There were, of course, festivities for Speech Day, which poor Prosper would miss. And the *Eton and Harrow match* – Cricket at Lord's – the highlight of the summer, he had to miss as well :

July 9 Friday   Lords. Was up in ward. Yates (another boy in the sick room) left. 1st day Harrow & Eton match. Harrow 85, Eton 141 on 1st innings.
July 10 Saturday 2nd day of Harrow & Eton match. Eton won. Harrow 175 in 2nd innings.

'Lord's' in those days was always a terrific social occasion, with all the mothers and sisters dressed in their best, and people who had them used their coaches – not modern motor-coaches, but fine four-in-hands or brakes, which were open-topped, with a lot of seats for a big party and extravagant picnic hampers. I don't think, even in those days, many actually *drove up* in the coaches, these were to Cut a Dash, traditionally impressive: they would have driven up in the Rollses and Daimlers and Bentleys, as those were the sort of cars the people with coaches did drive in.

There were always a lot of very fine refreshments at Lord's. Our great-uncle Wallace Hornby, at whose instigation Prosper had gone to Harrow, was a member of the MCC and used to give us tickets for Lord's. Our mother, with Guiny, did not go that year. She thought that without Prosper it wasn't worth the bother. But Uncle Wallace always went until he got too old, and Auntie Lilian and Uncle John had already planned to come up from Salop for it: so they kept to these arrangements, and took me: all of us staying at the Langham, which was quite a good, rather old-fashioned hotel in those days, around where the BBC landed later. Eric came with us, joining us each day at the Cricket Ground and staying the night at Mall Chambers. His parents did not attend the match.

I was very much aggrieved when Auntie Lilian wrote to my mother after these festivities to say that *Uncle John* was aggrieved that I paid no attention to him at Lord's – when *he* was standing me the salmon and champagne and the ballet in the evening – because I was too occupied in 'enjoying wild flirtations with Eric'. Her handwriting was absolutely terrible, and she swore that she had only written '*mild* flirtations' – a more likely definition for the confines of a cricket match. But of course we hadn't been flirting at all, only having some absorbing conversation about books, as usual. Equally of course, Prosper and Nors had a good bit of comment to make, and lost no opportunity later of asking us how our wild flirtations were getting on. Which had no effect whatever on Eric and me: we thought it very funny.

It must have been some time between the Easter and Summer holidays that the Blairs gave up 36 St Marks Road for good. Mr Blair stayed on a bit at Henley, living at the Golf Club, and it is recorded that Marjorie married Humphrey Dakin in July 1920. I have no recollection of this event. We were not asked to the wedding, so perhaps it was a very quiet one in London? The young couple lived in Mall Chambers after they were married, but I think in a flat of their own.

For the summer holidays Prosper records on 16 July:

> Came home by 12.20 from Paddington. Arrived about 1.45 in time for lunch.

And on Thursday 22 July:

> Heard from Auntie Lilian that Eric could come to Ticklerton in Aug so wrote to him to ask if he would like to come.

We note that there is no mention of Eric till 22 July, when Prosper *writes* to him. This bears out the first letter in the *Collected Essays* (Vol 1 p 33) to Steven Runciman from Polperro, dated '?August 1920?'. Presumably Eric spent the first part of the holidays in Cornwall and after that went to Maidensgrove. Prosper has noted on the address page of his diary: 'Eric Blair, 5 Horseshoes, Maidensgrove.' I imagined perhaps they might have had rooms at the village Pub: but, on conferring with Avril, she tells me:

> I do remember our holiday at Maidensgrove, where we were staying in a rather derelict cottage, rented, I imagine. I remember Eric building a sort of hut in the woods, made up of saplings laced with bracken. Unfortunately he called it 'Aston Villa'!! The name made with pebbles outside the entrance. I suppose it was the wrong team, as the local boys tore it down during the night.

Maidensgrove is on the other side of Henley, about four or five miles to the north-west not far from Nettlebed and Stonor, and so seven or eight miles from Shiplake. This was much further for Eric to bicycle than from St Marks Road, only a mile and a half from Quarry House, so he did not come over so often.

I saw very little of him during the 1920 summer holidays: by the time he got to the neighbourhood, I had left it to stay with Gran Finlay. Prosper records, for August:

4 Wednesday	Billy still here. [*Billy Wood, son of a friend of our Mother's who lived in London: a year or two older than I was.*] Went to Reading to Cinema. Jacintha went to Bournemouth. [*The two boys saw me off at Reading West station.*]
7 Saturday	Had letter from Eric to say he would come over on Monday and bring his 12-bore.
9 Monday	Eric came over for the day & brought his gun. Went out shooting but did not get much.
11 Wednesday	Went to Quarritts Farm with Eric. Only shot 4 rabbits & a pigeon. Went to Maidensgrove in evening.
12 Thursday	Shot at Maidensgrove with Eric but did not get anything. Came back in evening.
14 Saturday	Eric came over & we shot. Wargrave Regatta.
18 Wednesday	Eric came over for the day but it was too wet to shoot. Made chemicals experiments instead.
23 Monday	Jacintha is coming back tomorrow after 3 weeks stay in Bournemouth.
24 Tuesday	Eric came over. We made nitro-glycerin & gun cotton but the nitro-glycerin would not precipitate.
26 Thursday	Eric came over for the day. We tried to make nitro-Glycerin & got some ice to do it with. We packed.
27 Friday	Went to Ticklerton by 10.40 from Reading. Fished after tea & in evening. Got 17 perch & 1 eel weight 1 lb 6 oz. [*Note: Eric and I went to Ticklerton too, we are both mentioned later in the diary, and Prosper says 'we' packed: but Guiny did not come with us. In the Fishing Register at the end of the diary Eric is recorded as catching 8 perch on August 27th.*]
28 Saturday	Fished & shot. Caught 8 perch & shot 1 pigeon. [*Eric is recorded as catching 1 perch and shooting 1 crow.*]

29 Sunday	Fished most of the day. Caught a good many perch but no eels or trout. [*By the Register, Prosper caught 6 and Eric 9 perch on 29th.*]
30 Monday	Went out shooting with & without Ted Hall. I got 10 rabbits. Did not fish at all.
31 Tuesday	Went out riding in morning. In afternoon went out shooting with Ted & got 4 rabbits. [*By the Register, Eric got 3 rabbits.*]

Monday, 30 August is the sole day on which Eric is not recorded as having shot anything, or caught anything. I think it must have been the celebrated one-and-only occasion on which I went out shooting. As I remember, it was a lovely sunny day – *too* sunny, presumably to fish, as Prosper records, 'did not fish at all,' and Eric thought it would be nice for me to accompany them : naturally I did not carry a gun myself. When we returned, Uncle John made some comment on the fact that Prosper had a bag of ten rabbits whereas Eric was rabbitless. Prosper gave a rather surly explanation : 'Well, what else would you expect? *I* went out shooting with the dog – of course I got ten rabbits. *Eric* only went out shooting with Jacintha – I don't believe he even *tried* to shoot anything, he was just talking to her all the time.'

Eric might not have been *quite* so keen on killing things as was Prosper. While they shot, I usually led a Social Life with Auntie Lilian, visiting various neighbours.

The diary continues for September :

1 Wednesday	Went out shooting most of the day. Got 10 rabbits in all. I got 2, Eric 3.
2 Thursday	Eric & I went out shooting in morning & afternoon. I got 4 rabbits & he got 1.
3 Friday	Went out shooting in Edge Wood in morning. Got 2 rabbits. Went out with Ted in evening. Eric shot 2 rabbits.
4 Saturday	Eric left in morning. Jacintha & Auntie Lilian went to Shrewsbury. [*Incidentally seeing him*

off.] Took pony saddle back. Went out shooting. Got 8 rabbits.

10 Friday   Came back to Shiplake by train arr. in time for tea. Found Uncle Dudie waiting so went to cinema. [*He evidently took us*.]

No further mention of Eric, so presumably the Maidensgrove visit was over and the Blairs had returned to Mall Chambers, as on Friday, 17 September Prosper writes:

Went up to town & to The Skin Game with Eric. Then went on to Harrow, & arrived about 7 p.m.

Starting the Christmas holidays, he says, on Monday, 20 December:

Came home about 7.15. Went to Natural History Museum & Olympia Fair with Eric.

On Christmas Eve, our mother married Nors, her Faithful Dobbin. (*Vanity Fair* was the first book I ever read, after I had mastered the *O.X. Ox Book*, that excellent Macmillan's Primer, a red book with illustrations by Charles Robinson, when I was five. Prosper and Guiny could not read till they were nearly seven, because they were taught out of the *C.A.T. Cat Book*, Dales' blue primer, which taught phonetically. English is *not* a phonetic language, and it is idiocy to try to make things harder for children: Bernard Shaw was absolutely *past it* when he suggested his nonsensical new alphabet. But of course I spell with my eyes and not with my brain. Asked to spell something by voice, I can make no answer: I can only see, when it is written down, whether it is right or wrong. But is is normally unnecessary to 'spell out loud'.)

Prosper records for Friday, 24 December:

Mits & Nors married at Registry Office in Henley. We all went to the wedding.

Eric was in various places those holidays, but not with us. The last mention of him in Prosper's diary is Monday, 27 December : 'Jacintha had postcard from Eric.'

This postcard is no longer extant, and I can't remember if it was one of his milder saucy ones, or more probably a view of London, such as the Nelson Column or Big Ben, rather a convention with us. However, in its original envelope, addressed to Ticklerton and postmarked 'Paddington W.2. 12.45 pm 28 DEC 20' there still exists a 1920 letter to Prosper. It is simply headed :

28th
Usual

My dear Prosper,
    Thanks awfully for your invitation. I shall be very pleased to come & stay at Quarry House from the 17th to the end of the holidays. I expect this will find you at Ticklerton. My address will be

> Walnut Tree House
> Burstall
> nr. Ipswich

I go on Thursday. [*This would have been Thursday, 30 Dec. J.B.*] We are going to the Blue Lagoon this afternoon & The Beggar's Opera tomorrow. I hope you will have a good time in Shropshire. I must write & congratulate your mother on her marriage.

Yours
Eric

The 28th of December was a Tuesday. Prosper's diary notes for the following day, December 29th : 'Came to Ticklerton by 10.39 from Reading. Arrived about 4.30.'

The final entry is : 'Went over to shoot at Hills place at Marsh Brook. Altogether got 9 rabbits, 1 pheasant, 1 partridge, 1 snipe & 1 woodcock'.

A good mixed bag for Friday December 31st, the last day of the year.

Nineteen Twenty-One: Rickmansworth

JANUARY 1921 STARTS with another letter from Eric to Prosper, with the envelope again addressed to Ticklerton, postmarked Ipswich 1.30 p.m. 10 JA 21. The letter itself is undated, and headed:

Monday
Walnut Tree House
Burstall

My dear Prosper

Thanks for your letter. It was most awfully good your shooting the two snipe & the woodcock. You ought to get at least one of them stuffed, I think.

I have bought one of those big cage-rat traps. This place is overrun with rats. It is rather good sport to catch a rat & then let it out & shoot it as it runs. If it gets away I think one ought to let it go & not chase it. If they are threshing the corn while you are there, I should advise you to go, – it is well worth it. The rats come out in dozens. It is also rather sport to go at night to a corn-stack with an acetylene bicycle lamp

& you can dazzle the rats that are running along the side & whack at them, – or shoot them with a rifle. I rather wish I had my rifle here, as there are no rabbits.

Au revoir, please give my regards (or whatever it is) to your aunt & uncle & everyone.

> Yours
> Eric

This letter is written on pale blue linen-wove paper, in an envelope to match, a double-sheet: different from the cream single-sheet paper of the other two letters in matching envelopes that were written during these holidays, that he sent from London.

It had been arranged for Eric to stay at Quarry House before the boys went back to school, but this visit was unavoidably put off as Prosper got ill. Eric writes:

> Wednesday
> 23 Mall Chambers
> Nottinghill Gate W.8.

My dear Prosper

So sorry to hear you aren't well; it is rather a dismal way to end the holidays, but I suppose you won't mind much if you have to go back to school late. Mummie was going to have written to your mother, only she has been awfully busy lately. I didn't shoot anything much in Suffolk. All the rabbits had been wired; there were three covies of partridges there, but they were so wild that I could [n't] get a shot inside seventy yards. I trapped & shot a few rats. I hope you had a nice time in Shropshire. The shooting must have been just about at its best. I suppose Guinever was allowed to shoot this time.

I have got an idea of buying Turkish tobacco & making cigarettes of it, but it's awfully hard to get.

Well, au revoir; we are just going out. I hope you'll get better soon. Please remember me to everyone.

> Yours
> Eric

The envelope is addressed to Quarry House and postmarked Paddington W2 2.45 pm 19 Jan 21B. (19 January 1921 was a

Wednesday.) On it is a drinking-glass ring-mark, and a cryptic pencil note in Nors' handwriting,

'6 *p.m.* 21.1.21

102.1.'

which puzzled me at first, till I realised it must have been a note of Prosper's temperature when they began to be alarmed about him.

At first they thought he merely had a bad cold, or flu, but soon spots appeared and developed into such a bad attack of chickenpox that the doctor at one stage feared it might be smallpox. Prosper was so ill that it took him some time to recover and he was not able to go back to school that term.

When Eric came to stay in the Easter holidays, Prosper was convalescent, but his heart had been affected. The heart-specialist forbade his return at all to one of the School Houses. So just before the summer term the whole family was packed up and moved bodily to Harrow, in order that Prosper could be a *Home Boarder* (as they called day-boys) with his mother on the spot to be responsible for taking care of his health. We were therefore based on Harrow for the rest of Prosper's schooldays. He was not allowed to play games for several terms, which was bad luck on him as he was devoted to them and getting along quite nicely, with a place in the Torpids (the Junior teams). And any remote possibility of his following in the footsteps of his cricketing relative, old A. N. Hornby, was finished – Uncle Wallace had so much hoped for this that he was giving some financial support towards the school-fees: he had no sons or grandsons of his own.

For the summer term 1921 we rented a house called Wood-lands which belonged to the later celebrated Mrs Meyrick (not quite so celebrated then) and we all, including Eric, went to Lord's for the Eton and Harrow match.

The Blairs had parted with 36 St Marks Road, but not found another family home to replace it. So for the 1921 summer holidays, Mrs Blair with Eric and Avril shared a house called Glencroft at Rickmansworth with our mother and Nors and us three. Marjorie at times came down from London for the day or a weekend, but I don't recollect Mr Blair ever being there. I think he was house-hunting in Suffolk, staying with friends or relations to be near whom they eventually settled in Southwold.

1921 was a gloriously, unforgettably, hot summer, immediately brought to mind whenever we hear the tunes of the day. There was a gramophone that went with the house, and a large selection of records. Some may have been American or foreign, because when we got home we tried to buy them for ourselves and found them to be unobtainable. One fascinating piece was called *The Chinese Wedding Procession*, and my favourite of all was a *Chaconne* by Durand. Guiny and Avril were fonder of *I'm Forever Blowing Bubbles*, which appealed to their more tender years, and *The Stephanie Gavotte*. Guiny says she thinks that was the first we heard of *Poor Butterfly* : and it may have been. But for me *Poor Butterfly* is Magdalen and another summer.

Glencroft had a tennis-court, so a lot of tennis was played; and there was a stream bordering the meadows beyond the garden, with freshwater crayfish. Both Guiny and Avril remember some sort of bother with the River Warden over the crayfish : they didn't know they were trespassing. Fishing Rights Proper were rented, at the local reservoir, which were really rather a swindle. At the end of a long day, packing up to go home, Eric shouted across from his side of the water to Prosper at the other : 'I haven't caught anything – have you ?' To which Prosper shouted back : 'Not actually, but I've had one good bite.' The pleasure of fishing seemed to lie in the fishing itself and not in any end-product such as fish.

There was a billiard-hall in the village, called by the boys 'The Billiard Hell', where they occasionally played by themselves

– LADIES WERE NOT ALLOWED, according to conspicuous placards. I rather fancied myself at billiards, my one active game which I had practised a good bit at Phyllis: so they suggested adapting the old tag, 'These aren't ladies, they're only our sisters', but there was no relaxation of the rule.

We found many advantages at Glencroft, which was an exceedingly well-equipped house: a couple of bicycles had been left, which the boys found invaluable, and chickens which were conscientiously cared for mostly by Guiny and Nors. There was also quite a reasonable library, which contained several *Greyfriars Annuals*, on which we fell with hilarity. Greyfriars was new to me then, and I think equally new to Eric. He made use of the material, somewhat scathingly, in his 'Boys' Weeklies' (*Collected Essays*, Vol 1 pp 505/531, and *Horizon*, March 1940) to which Frank Richards made an unanswerable and witty reply in *Horizon* the following May. (Also in *Collected Essays*, Vol 1, pp 531/540). I don't think that Prosper and Eric ever read the *Gem* or the *Magnet*. Their periodicals were such magazines as the *Strand*, and the *Windsor* through which I think around that time a Dornford Yates serial was running. Eric didn't care for Dornford Yates: he said the characters were too improbable. But Prosper and I quite enjoyed him, and thought some of the characters rather like some of the people we met at Phyllis. Of course, Eric didn't care for Phyllis either.

* * * *

One of the strangest things in the *Orwell Mystique* is the apparent general incomprehension as to why he ever went to Burma, and the remarkable reason offered for his doing so.

If *Bones and Sons* is inscribed above the local butcher's shop, we are not surprised to see young Billy and Bertie Bones busily baronning the beef beside their father. If on our Solicitors' notepaper we read the heading: *Peabody Peabody Popinjay Cattermole and Peabody*, although Popinjay together with all the Peabodies would have departed from this world sometime in the eighteen-nineties if they are any normal firm of solicitors, we would quite naturally expect to see Charles Cattermole Junior rushing around with a briefcase completing his articles, or sedately seated in his father's office interviewing the less eminent clients. So how is it that it did not occur to anyone, very simply indeed, that Eric went to Burma to follow the Precept of his Papa?

In what is apparently a school textbook, *Animal Farm Notes*, by Howard Fink, published by Coles, the author states of Eric:

> At his graduation from Eton in 1921, when he might have gone on to University, he was advised by one of his teachers to join the civil service instead, and he was sent as a sergeant in the Indian Imperial Police, to Burma.

Says George Bott, editing *George Orwell: Selected Writings*, published by Heinemann:

> When the time came for him to leave Eton, Orwell did not take the normal step of going to a university, though he could probably have won a scholarship if he had wished. Mr Tom Hopkinson says that Orwell was advised by one of his tutors to find a job abroad, make plenty of money, and at the age of forty retire and choose whatever way of life appealed to him.

And a similar theory was put forward in the 1971 television programme, *The Road to the Left*: that he had gone into the Burmese Police in order to be able to retire, with great wealth, at *forty*.

It is an odd theory: Let us examine it.

According to the *Mystique*, George Orwell, when young, had suffered bitterly from the consciousness of his father's poverty: and we note that this alleged poverty was old Mr Blair's reward for having worked in the Indian Civil from the age of eighteen in 1875 until he retired at fifty-five in 1912, thirty-seven years later, on a pension so small that it was claimed to be inadequate to keep his family without being eked out by his retirement post at the Golf Club.

Had Mr Blair retired fifteen years earlier, instead of at fifty-five, presumably his pension would have been still smaller. So where is the wonderful opportunity, in the Indian Civil, of *retiring with great wealth at forty?* True, Mr Blair's branch, the Opium Department, was a different section from the Burmese Police. But would one expect to fare any *better* in the Burmese Police – except by very heavy involvement with graft? And Eric was emphatically not the stuff of which dishonest policemen are made. One would need to be a very dishonest Burmese Policeman indeed to be able to retire *with great wealth* at forty. Eric's father, with even better opportunities in the Opium Department had obviously not succumbed to them.

Of course the Drug Traffic in his day was another thing quite different from what it is now. The current cataclysm of drug addiction is genuinely incomprehensible to me: I like to be master of my own mind, and to get tangible value for money.

During the Rickmansworth holiday there were interminable conversations between our mother and Mrs Blair, united in deploring old Mr Blair's obstinate attitude regarding Eric's future. Indian Civil he had been himself, and Indian Civil was the only career he would tolerate for his son. It was the last thing Eric wanted, but the tramlines were laid down.

Our mother was very fond of Eric, and far more understanding of his wish to be an author than was his father. (She did a bit of writing herself, mostly short pieces of historical biography, some of which got into the *Cornhill* or *Chambers' Journal*: she only wrote two books – *Philippa's Adventures in Upside-down-land* when she was seventeen, a children's story in the style of Lewis Carroll, and *The Lady of Bleeding Heart Yard*, the life story of Lady Elizabeth Hatton, many years later.)

So when Mrs Blair sided with Eric in a desperate last-minute stand for a final last-minute chance of Oxford, our mother backed them up in some vigorous correspondence with old Mr Blair, strongly advocating that Oxford was 'the proper thing' for a boy. She told him that 'at whatever sacrifice' she was determined that Prosper should be given the opportunity. But Mr Blair was adamant: nothing could alter his own equal determination that Eric should *not*. Eric frequently sat in on these discussions, especially whenever an epistle from Mr Blair was read out, when he was not engaged in outdoor pursuits with the others. But as I very seldom fished and never played tennis, I heard most of them: and even more of Eric's own point of view, since he talked to me a good deal on the subject. We were rather in the habit of going for country walks.

There was quite a country air to Rickmansworth in those days. I remember one particular way we went, along a lane which was rather hot and dusty in that very hot summer, so we kept to the shady side of the hedges in the cornfields. He was probably thinking of these cornfields when he wrote me another poem: I certainly thought of them when I read it. We were in the Glencroft drawing-room, with the gramophone playing Durand's *Chaconne*, when he gave me this quatrain to which, on the lower part of the same page, I put a reply:

Eric: Friendship and love are closely intertwined,
         My heart belongs to your befriending mind:
         But chilling sunlit fields, cloud-shadows fall —
         My love can't reach your heedless heart at all.

Jacintha: By light
          Too bright
          Are dazzled eyes betrayed:
          It's best
          To rest
          Content in tranquil shade.

Typical of both of us, Eric with his straightforward, ten-syllable couplets, and me chopping up the same metre into shorter lines with extra rhymes to them, which I thought more fun to do and more singable. It is because I sang this song to the so-favourite chaconne that I remember it so well: it had to be sung: 'But chilling sunlit fields, cloud-shadows *sometimes* fall', to comply with the tune. And it was reversed for the second part, and adapted:

> *It's best*
> *To rest*
> *Content in tranquil shade:*
> *By light*
> *Too bright*
> *Are dazzled eyes betrayed –*

> So,
> *Chilling sunlit fields*, sometimes *cloud-shadows fall –*
> Although
> *Your love can't reach my heedless heart at all,*
> Still
> *Friendship and love are closely intertwined –*
> Will
> *Heart belong to true befriending mind?*

I have not heard that *Chaconne* played since we left Rickmansworth, but I can still hear it in my mind.

There is music in my mind most of the time, other people's or my own. It's not surprising that Beethoven didn't care inconsolably that he was deaf. I can *hear* my *Flower Song*, with a whole orchestra, and I can see the scene: the woman singing to her child, with the wraiths outside. Just as I can hear the Durand *Chaconne* that was *really* heard so many years ago, and as I can see the drawing-room at Glencroft with Eric in our young, and for me unclouded, friendship.

Friendship and love are closely intertwined
My heart belongs to your befriending mind.

By any standards, those are good lines: simple and good.

*   *   *

All these three poems of Eric's that I remember have cloud-images in them: prophetic, perhaps. And the heart-and-mind contrast was a favourite theme of his. I was reminded of it by the glorious 'Heart and Mind' of Edith Sitwell:

Said the Lion to the Lioness, 'When you are amber dust –
No more a raging fire like the heart of the sun
(No liking but all lust) –
Remember still the flowering of the amber blood and bone
The rippling of bright muscles like a sea,
Remember those rose-prickles of bright paws
Though we shall mate no more
Till the fire of that sun and the moon-cold bone are one.

I didn't read this till my Aunt and Uncle Burke gave me the book, newly published, for Christmas 1945. But as soon as I saw it, I thought of Eric and wished he could have enjoyed it with me.

Regarding clouds, there is another poem I wish we could have shared the pleasure of. I have never been able to retrace this, since reading it some time in the 1930's: so if anyone recognises it, and can tell me where to find it, it would be nice to be told. It *might* have been in some historical novel by Marjorie Bowen – a rather unlikely *milieu*:

The clouds were tangled in the trees
They broke the boughs and spoiled the fruit.
The dreamer knows what the dreamer sees –
You play spades and I'll follow suit.

119

If I've lost, it is no matter.
If I've won, it's naught at all.
The wind will chill
And the sun will flatter
And the red earth fill
The mouths of all.

(The lightning flashed through blinding rain
It woke the trees in flames of fire,)
The dreamer rent his dream in twain
And cast his cards in the bitter mire.
If I've won, it is no matter.
If I've lost, it's naught at all —
The wind will chill
And the sun will flatter
And the red earth fill
The mouths of all.

I am uncertain of the first two lines of the second verse, so have had to improvise, and there may have been another verse. Of all the poems I've ever read, this one and the first verse of the 'Lion and Lioness' are what I'd have most liked to have written myself. I don't know that they were really Eric's type of poetry – he inclined more to the regular form and the matter-of-fact. But I'd have liked to have shown them to him, all the same.

In the *Collected Essays* (Vol 4, pp 474/475) he gives a good exposition on poetry to George Woodcock who had sent him some verses to read:

> I think you should make your mind up a bit better on the subject of rhyme. Part of the time you use ordinary rhymes, but a good deal of the time assonances like thought-white, hours-fears etc; I must say I am against this kind of rhyme, which seems to me only, as it were, an intellectual rhyme,

existing on paper because we can see that the final consonant is the same. The lack of rhymes in English is a very serious difficulty and gets more serious all the time, as familiar rhymes get more and more hackneyed, but I have always felt that if one is to use imperfect rhymes it would be better to make the vowel sound and not the consonant the same, e.g. open-broken, fate-shape, sound to me more like rhymes than eye-voice, town-again, and so forth. However, I'm no judge of such things.

Unnecessary modesty from one who was the 'Stern Critic' at thirteen, now merely stating clear and obvious fact.

This letter was written on 24 April 1948, when *Vers* was less *Libre* than it is now. Currently it is often not so much *libre* as lunatic. If we open the pages of the poor old *Poetry Review* – at one time so adventurous, but now largely a bore – we discover that to be *too* groovey is to be utterly stuck in a groove: we find a superfluity of what might appear to be fugitive wodges from the wastepaper basket, apparently printed by mistake, instead of being left in the *bin* along with the other asylum inmates. Rhyming is never *obligatory*: so why, if the exigencies of the English language preclude a rhyme or the writer is unable to think of one, remain in a rhyming rut? I thoroughly agree with Eric that such monstrosities as thought-white, hours-fears are emphatically a 'kind of rhyme' to be against. I would say they were unpardonable. If poetry is *supposed* to rhyme, it should: but not necessarily too obviously. I rather like interval-rhymes in alternate verses, and irregular lines, although the rhythm should be perfect. If he *needed* thought-white, why not put them in different lines? For example:

> He had a thought:
> His thought was white.
> He thought it ought
> To last the night.

But dark the hours
As darker fears
Of darkest powers
Assailed his ears –
With staring eyes
And soundless voice,
For bright sunrise
He will rejoice –
With speed, to town
He'll take the train –
Although his hosts bear credit and renown
He never will come down
To stay with them again.

We might call it 'Perhaps it was only an Owl; or Uninvited Guest' – nicely ambiguous, as it might refer to the miserable city-dweller, unaccustomed to the turbulence of the country, who had unexpectedly parked himself on reluctant hosts, or to the actual owl, quite equally unexpected. Perhaps DARKEST POWERS might be in capitals.

All poetry did not find equal favour in Eric's eyes at all times. That August at Rickmansworth he gave Guiny his Everyman copy of Milton, in which he had previously inscribed for his own benefit, following the contours of the endpaper design:

E. A. Blair K. S.
Bought this book   Much against his will   For the study of
Milton   a poet   for whom   he had   no   love: but
he was   compelled   to study   him   or abandon
English Extra Studies   which not being   Commendable to him
He was compelled to   Squander three and sixpence
On this nasty little book.

Possibly he had a *surfeit* of Milton for English Extra Studies: he speaks appreciatively of him in 'Why I Write' (*Collected Essays*, Vol 1, pp 24/25) up to a point:

When I was about sixteen I suddenly discovered the joy of

mere words, i.e. the sounds and associations of words. The lines from *Paradise Lost*

> *So hee with difficulty and labour hard*
> *Moved on: with difficulty and labour hee*

which do not now seem to me so very wonderful, sent shivers down my backbone; and the spelling 'hee' for 'he' was an added pleasure.

Certainly those particular two lines do not seem the most inspiring of Milton. But of course there can be a delight in words simply as words: I feel exactly the same sort of pleasure over what I still consider to be a supremely exquisite line of Clough's:

> *Home, Rose, and home – Provence and La Palie.*

It *is* beautiful, although it is merely a catalogue of cows. But in their very names are the meadows starred with buttercups, and the almost-twilight sky.

Eric says he made his discovery at sixteen, and *anything* may for *something* be a catalyst. He was eighteen when he gave his Milton to Guiny, having by then himself no doubt moved on.

Guiny was very pleased with this present: she had a rather heavy taste in literature. She wrote to me, the following month, on the old-fashioned pale grey mottled notepaper that was always used there:

TICKLERTON COURT
CHURCH STRETTON
SHROPSHIRE

September 20th 1921

My dear Gal –

Gal, indeed! Sauce from a child of fourteen to her senior sister of twenty! But Guiny, by the time she was fourteen, was two or three inches taller than I was: so each of us could, with justification, refer to the other as her *little* sister. Anyway, that was how she started.

My dear Gal

Many thanks for your long and interesting letter which I had the joy of receiving this same morning . . .

I fear that truthfulness is not one of your strongest points. – You can guess that I am referring to the cheese. The block from which your piece was cut has not taken it into its worthy head to cause such disturbances at a piecefull [sic] meal table and yours being a 'chip of the old block' I cannot immagine it to have swerved so far from parental authority as to behave its self in the way you describe before such select company as your own. [*It was always the custom at Ticklerton to have a WHOLE Stilton, which was kept beforehand for some time in the cellar to mature, with Grandpapa at intervals pouring PORT into it, by a small deep hole: Proper Stilton is one of my favourite cheeses so it was also the custom, if Guiny went up without me, for her to send me a piece as consolation. But evidently this time I had considered it too mature. J.B.*]

Peveril of the Peak is in three volumes, two of which I have nearly finished, that is to say I have quite finished one and nearly finished the other. It is a splendid work. Apt, I fear, to take the side of the Stuarts, but well worth reading even for a Roundhead. [*Needless to say that Guiny was a Cromwellian, while I was a Cavalier. J.B.*] As you do not appear to have read it, and being after 6 pm I no longer entertain hopes of catching the evening post with this letter, I will give you a brief summary . . . (*She does so for 3 pages*) . . . I have no doubt I have not got the full gist of things now, but I would have my way and write a summary to satisfy my restless pen.

"Give e'en a dunce the employment he desires
And he soon finds the talent he requires."

That's Cowper – he's one of the best of poets. I've just found a book of his poetical works, and it's all I can do to drag myself away from them. They quite throw Milton into the shade.

I have read also, under Auntie Lilian's recommendation, some of Aytoun's Lays, which are certainly not bad.

I am also taken with some lines of Byron, but with the last-named poet it is only occasionally that I hit upon pieces that I like, while with Cowper all is excellent. I think I shall get some of his lines by heart.

I have got too much to read yet, but am working steadily at Scott. My Gal, I'm working through the row, you know the shelf, it has about 46 volumes and I am quite a way along it, though I passed over the Bride of Lammermoor and a few others. . .

On Sunday we dressed in our best and went to Church. It was the 18th of September, the 3rd anniversary of Auntie Lilian and Uncle John's wedding. We returned after Church to a meal of roast duck etc: etc; and I forget what the pudding was and drank everybodies health in champagne and port. During the meal, Grandpapa, who had just had his glass refilled with champagne, said that he thought that anniversaries were very good things. This did not fail to draw a laugh from every one of the Company.

After lunch Uncle John and Auntie Lilian went for a nap and I read Peveril of the Peak. After tea we went for an excellent motor drive and took Maggie with us.

We went along the Wall Road and over the hill from which you can see the Wrekin and turned right and went through several villages one of which I believe was called Shipton. We stopped and looked at the outside view of several old houses one I believe was Shipton Hall. It was of the Elizabethan style of Architecture and stood on the right hand side of the road as we passed. It was separated from a small Church by what is known as the Ghost Walk, which as its name implies is supposed to be haunted. I do not know whether you have seen or heard of the place I am speaking of?

We drove round in a kind of semi-circle coming down through the Edge Wood, past Roberts farm and across the brook to Ticklerton, getting home just in time to change for supper. [*We always had to change in the evening – even just for cold Sunday Supper; on weekdays there was Dinner in the evenings, with several courses, even if only just the family were at home. But on Sundays the main meal was in the middle of the day, to give the maids a rest in the evening and go to Church if they wanted to. J.B.*]

Today (Wednesday) a night having passed since I commenced this weary letter which I shall soon despatch. This morning the hounds came but we did not see them very close. Great excitement prevailed and we were continually dashing to the front door on false alarms. –

Togo [the spaniel] and especially Kitty [the mare] were greatly delighted, the latter ran round the meadow like mad when she heard the hunters shouting – this of course wasted a great deal of our time . . . the Old Brougham was brought round and many other things done. But I must away just now and ask Auntie Lilian if I can help her in any way . . . I have no time to write more . . .

Much love
Guiny

Ancient and Modern were mingled at Ticklerton : although there was a family Ford – driven by Uncle John – Grandpapa still preferred, and stuck to, his horse-drawn vehicles. The Old Brougham was for larger parties and wet weather, the dog-cart for two or three people on finer days and for speed – not that old Kitty (the one remaining horse) was of an age to be very speedy by that time, and when after outliving Grandpapa she finally departed to the Horses' Heaven she was not replaced. The Landau had gone before them, shortly after the death of Grandmama.

The envelope of this letter of Guiny's is addressed to me at West Hill Hotel, Harrow-on-the-Hill : so we were at that time evidently between houses. For the autumn term we rented Rowney, which also had an interesting library. There were a lot of old bound volumes of *Punch* and glossy weeklies like the *Illustrated London News* : in which it was interesting to find some stage photographs of *A White Man* and notice what a lot I remembered from the time RAB took me to it on one of the matinée treats.

Before Christmas we moved into the pleasant Oldfield House, which belonged to the Lunns, and remained there for the rest of Prosper's schooldays. The dog Bobby came with us to Harrow, but after the disappearance of Quillie my mother had sold Toto, Mannie's successor as Quillie's second husband. She had kept one last kitten from Quillie's last litter : but when we left

Shiplake this cat Kizatesh Sultana was given to Uncle Dudie, who re-christened her Bessie (a rather far-fetched abbreviation of 'Teshie' for Kizatesh) and made a great pet of her for the several years of her life.

12

Eric and Sex

IF, ON GLANCING through the list of chapter headings, any inhabitants of Permissive 1974 turn hastily to read this one first in the hope of delicate (or indelicate) revelations, I must warn them that so far as Eric and I were concerned, sex resembled the seacoast of Bohemia. There wasn't any. The subject, as such, was one that we neither discussed nor practised.

In *Such Such Were the Joys* (*Collected Essays*, Vol 4, pp 403/404) Eric says of himself:

> At five or six, like many children, I had passed through a phase of sexuality. My friends were the plumber's children up the road, and we used sometimes to play games of a vaguely erotic kind. One was called 'playing at doctors', and I remember getting a faint but definitely pleasant thrill from holding a toy trumpet, which was supposed to be a stethoscope, against a little girl's belly. About the same time I fell deeply in love, a far more worshipping kind of love than I have ever felt for anyone since, with a girl named Elsie at the convent school which I attended. She seemed to me grown-up so I suppose must have been fifteen. After that, as so often happens, all sexual feelings seemed to go out of me for many

years. At twelve I knew more than I had known as a young
child, but I understood less, because I no longer knew the
essential fact that there is something pleasant in sexual acti-
vity. Between seven and fourteen the whole subject seemed
to be uninteresting, and when for some reason I was forced to
think of it, disgusting.

And, further, on page 420 :

When I fell in love with Elsie I took her to be grown-up. I
met her again, when I was thirteen, and she, I think, must have
been twenty-three; she now seemed to me to be a middle-aged
woman, somewhat past her best. And the child thinks of growing old as an almost obscene calamity, which for some mysterious reason will never happen to itself.

If 'Elsie' was neither a pseudonym – like other characters in
THE JOYS – nor Miss Elsie Mallinson, then perhaps she might
have been Elsie Gorell-Barnes, daughter of Sir Frederick Gorell-
Barnes, who lived not far from Mrs Irving : the only Elsie in
the neighbourhood. She was about the right age with the right
name. As our respective families were only acquaintances
rather than intimate friends, I remember very little about her
except that she was pretty and had a brother who was killed
in the War : I don't think there was any sister, but she might
have had one or two younger brothers – it was all so long ago.
I have a *very* vague idea that it was on the Gorell-Barnes'
recommendation that Prosper and I were sent to the Henley
Convent School.

But if Eric fell in love with 'Elsie' at a precocious five years
old, and out again at thirteen when he rediscovered her to be
an antique crone rising all of twenty-three, he did not inform
me of this episode. This is not to suggest it did not happen :
both natural reticence and politic tact might well have deterred
him from mentioning it.

In this same essay, on page 419 we read :

Looking back on my own childhood, after the infant years were over, I do not believe I felt love for any mature person except my mother, and even her I did not trust, in the sense that shyness made me conceal most of my real feelings from her. Love, the spontaneous, unqualified emotion of love was something I could only feel for people who were young. Towards people who were old – and remember that old to a child means over thirty, or even twenty-five – I could feel reverence, respect, admiration or compunction, but I seemed cut off from them by a veil of fear and shyness mixed with physical distaste.

The operative word here is 'mature', which would not apply to us, his contemporaries: Marjorie, the eldest, would still be under his lower limit of twenty-five, even when he departed for Burma – by which time he himself was nineteen and no longer a child. When he was young, there is no doubt his mother *was* the only adult he loved in the absolute sense: and part of the 'cutting-off-veil' might have been due, together with the physical distaste, to the sudden impact of a hitherto unknown and unusually elderly father when Eric was at the inexperienced but observant age of eight.

The Unknown Orwell (pp 232/233) quotes of Brenda Salkeld:

whom he met in the Autumn of 1928 at Southwold, where she was the gym mistress at St Felix School . . . She came to the conclusion that he did not really understand people, women in particular, that he could not give himself. And while no doubt some of this grew out of their immediate circumstances, there clearly was a quality of 'apartness' and abstraction about him that many had noticed before, a short-circuiting of the emotions, a failure to connect . . . 'He didn't really like women', was Miss Salkeld's verdict. 'I used to bring up the women who I thought were good writers and he would occasionally praise their writing, but he used to say that it stuck in his throat to have to do it.'

Perhaps it wasn't very helpful for Miss Salkeld to have been a gym mistress when first they became acquainted. Conditioned, as a boy, to my constant tenet that 'games for girls were ghastly', Eric might have had a subconscious barrier against someone who made them a career. Their friendship might have been more easily flowing if she had taught something else – languages or literature?

Nevertheless, it seems to have been a long-lasting and useful friendship – over twenty years later, in a letter to Richard Rees headed 'Cranham 25 April 1949', Eric makes a reference to her:

> When Brenda comes I am going to get her to make up some parcels for me & send home some of the books which are piling up fearfully. (*Collected Essays*, Vol 4, p 560.)

If Miss Salkeld is still alive, whether or not still Miss Salkeld, I should rather like to meet her.

By the time she came on the scene, his attitude might have altered, but in all the years that *we* knew him, there was never a shadow of a reason to suppose that he 'didn't really like women'. And Avril says (in a letter dated 18.5.73):

> As regards Eric and women, I don't think he really disliked them. In fact I can think of more women with whom he was friendly & seemed fond of than I can men. The fact is, he was an aloof, rather remote person, especially after his return from Burma. I always found it strange that, although no hint of sex ever appeared in his conversation, his books were often quite lewd. This may have been a left over Victorianism inherited from our parents who never mentioned sex either.

Of course, friendship and love are not *always* closely intertwined.

It is true that Eric was an undemonstrative boy. He was the absolute reverse of the super-susceptible Prosper, whose all-embracing affections from the age of seven were fleetingly distracted by every pretty girl he met – and he went right out of his way to meet pretty girls: it was awfully hard to keep pace with the swift succession. Perhaps one of the reasons the two boys were such good friends was that in this particular tournament Eric was never competing.

But Eric was certainly not a misogynist. In his home life there were three women: his mother and two sisters, with whom he always seemed perfectly happy even if he wasn't cuddling them all day long, as against one man, his father, often absent and with whom he was not on such congenial terms. With Prosper's sisters, he was as friendly as he was with Prosper – there was no attitude of 'Let us chaps go off by ourselves and leave these awful girls behind.' If we did not invariably do the same things together at the same time, it was because we had our separate preferences. I did not go shooting with them, when he shot with Prosper and Guiny, because I hated wild things to be killed: but he did not despise me for this – he simply accepted it as a different point of view, just as he accepted that Prosper did not specially care for literature. For the heavier type he congregated with Guiny (Milton, Scott, etc) and for the less weighty, and with his own writings, he came for companionship to me. I did a lot of sewing, and Eric – a typical boy – was not interested in sewing, but he frequently talked, or read aloud to me while I sewed.

On occasion he saw more of our mother, who was at home all the time, than of his own mother when she was away working. I do not say he *loved* my mother, but he certainly got on extremely well with her, as he did with Auntie Lilian. They were both fond of him and considered him to be an interesting, intelligent boy, with whom they conversed at adult level. He spoke quite affectionately of his Limouzin aunts, and the only woman I remember him *not* particularly keen on was Mrs Wilkes. Even for her, I think at the time the description would be more accurately 'not particularly keen' than 'loathing ferociously', or whatever impression is given by *The Joys*. So of the women and girls he knew well in our young day, he would have been *for* about nine or ten, and *against* only one – this without counting the problematical 'Elsie': I don't know quite where we should place her – with childish worship balanced by thirteen-year-old disenchantment, perhaps a *draw*?

All this seems to refer more to a general attitude to women rather than to sex.

Since we never discussed it, I do not *know* what Eric's views were on sex: but without anything being actually said, I got the impression that it was *taboo* because he thought it improper and therefore unmentionable – so he didn't mention it. I didn't consider it was necessarily improper, but I *did* think it was private – so I didn't mention it either.

Theoretically, there could have been plenty to mention. The bachelor Uncle Dudie had a bachelor section in his library over which, as soon as I could read, I had free range – like every other bookshelf in our family's various households; though all did not have the same contents as Uncle Dudie's. I would not suggest that the whole section were especially pornographic: but the most innocent infant could hardly fail to become aware of what was what, with the run of these shelves on which Uncle Dudie's Greeks had a great variety of words for all sorts of things. But, most tactfully, among all the books we talked about, I never talked about Uncle Dudie's more curious ones to Eric. I didn't think he would quite appreciate them.

I was not a pornographic child, so I selected my reading matter discriminately, concentrating on what I thought was interesting. I had no wish to substitute practice for theory, neither did I bother with anything that seemed just crude, repetitive, or dull – or sometimes all three. There was a book of limericks of which I took a poor view: even at ten or twelve I saw no wit in something the *supposed* wit of which was the dragging in of a couple of four-letter words and a bit of anatomy by their tails – all struggling and screaming because they hadn't been provided with efficient rhymes or allowed to scan.

There is a more entertaining selection in the modern *Pan Book of Limericks*. I did not find *one* in that printed-in-Paris tome which was worth remembering, let alone repeating to Eric, though, in a repeatable form, it was a form we often used.

My own favourite of the Ancient Classics is still :

> *There was a young Curate of Salisbury*
> *Whose habits were halisbury-scalisbury.*
> *He wandered through Hampshire*
> *Without any pampshire*
> *Till his Bishop compelled him to walisbury.*

Eric and I concocted several of our own that I've forgotten, but a *chumly* one on which we collaborated together is more memorable :

> *A nervous young fellow named Cholmondeley*
> *Found his hard-boiled egg sandwich too crolmondeley.*
> *But his hostess, Miss Moore,*
> *Hated crumbs on the floore –*
> *So she didn't put up with him dolmondeley.*

We had a bit of discussion as to whether *Miss Maw* should have hated crumbs on the *Flaw*, but decided that to be consistent the lady's name merited priority for pronunciation not-as-spelt.

Comparatively recently I thought of quite a pretty one :

> *Some Persons from Charing Cross Rd.*
> *Removed to another abd.*
> *They explained that a St.*
> *With police on the bt.*
> *Was not part of their own Highway Cd.*

This really *is* rather pretty, because the Persons are so purely non-committal. They might be naughty girls, or still naughtier boys, or petty pilferers from the tuppenny tray at Foyles, or –

in permissive 1974 and in proximity to Soho – more likely a couple of Godfathers.

I never heard, or saw any sign, that Eric was interested in *rude* limericks – subtlety set our standard – but from the earliest time I knew him, he had a rather parallel hobby of Saucy Postcards. This dated from St Cyprian's days: at Eastbourne such cards would have been prevalent. It is interesting to see this hobby re-echoed years later in 'The Art of Donald McGill' (*Collected Essays*, Vol 2, p 183 and *Horizon*, Feb. 1942 and elsewhere).

Eric kept his collection in an album, which travelled from Rose Lawn to 36 St Marks Road, and he always showed me the visible new additions in subsequent holidays. 'Visible', because also in this album was a manilla postcard-sized envelope which he strictly forbade me ever to open. He said I wouldn't care for the cards inside because they were 'too vulgar'. How they could have been any more vulgar than some of those which were boldly displayed in the body of the book, I cannot imagine: but most honourably I never attempted to find out. Perhaps they were Feelthy Peectures? But I shouldn't have thought Eric would have collected those, or if he had, that he would have kept them in such a prominent place with such a prestigious prohibition.

Possibly a hint of Eric's attitude to sex might have been given by his attitude towards his saucy postcards: those open to the light of day in the album were rather weeded out into sheep and goats. I recognise descriptions of one or two of them in 'The Art of Donald McGill', where some of his comments and conclusions may explain how, in his youth, the *taboo* impression may have been given.

For example, he writes (*Collected Essays*, Vol 2, p 189):

A young bridegroom is shown getting out of bed the morning after his wedding night. 'The first morning in our own little home, darling!' he is saying; 'I'll go and get the milk and paper and bring you a cup of tea.' Inset is a picture of the front door-step; on it are four newspapers and four bottles of milk. This is obscene if you like, but it is not immoral.

Well, no. If they are *married*, it cannot be immoral, but it can hardly be obscene either. The fact that they found their honey-moon so delicious that four days seemed like an evening gone might bring a sympathetic smile to the postman, but he would think them not so much obscene as fortunate.

For real obscenity one must go to that *awful* exposition of Eric's own – Chapter 3, part 1, in *A Clergyman's Daughter* – where Dorothy spends the night with a mass of mixed tramps piled up in newspapers on a bench in Trafalgar Square. It is utterly revolting. How Eric came to write it is incomprehensible: but he seems to be *pleased* with it. He writes to Brenda Salkeld on 7 March 1935 (*Collected Essays*, Vol 1, p 174):

> I sent you off your copy of *A Clergyman's Daughter* last night. As you will see, it is tripe, except for chap 3 part 1, which I am pleased with, but I don't know whether *you* will like it.

Dorothy herself, of course, is incomprehensible. Granted that, given far-fetched circumstances, she might lose her memory and become penniless, *how* could she involve herself with a swarm of stinking tramps? We are told, in Chapter 5:1, that when, in a railway carriage, 'Mr Warburton tightened his grip and pulled her against him . . . a wave of disgust and deadly fear went through her and her entrails seemed to shrink and freeze.' Fair enough, if she was a thin spinster allergic to fat bachelors. But if the washed and well-meaning Mr Warburton – who was far kinder to her than the silly girl deserved – filled her with repulsion, then *what* was she doing, rolling about with the tramps?

So many of Eric's characters in so many of his novels are so strangely slanted to squalor. He seems obsessed by the sordid and the smelly. Look at the seduction scene in *Keep the Aspi-*

distra Flying: it is so very unlikely Rosemary would have succumbed to it.

His novels appear to prove that Brenda Salkeld was right
when she said that when *she* knew him he didn't understand
women and (by then) didn't really like them. This seems to be
corroborated by a snide sentence of his own, in *Collected
Essays*, Vol 1, p 256, on Conrad: 'One of the surest signs of his
genius is that women disliked his books.' (*New English Weekly*,
23 July 1936: Review.)

As I was copying out this sentence, my eye fell on another
on the opposite page in a letter to Henry Miller dated 26 August 1936, *à propos Black Spring*: 'I like very much your meditation beginning in a public urinal.' Why meditate in a public
urinal? What an awfully uncomfortable and inauspicious environment – and probably smelly as well, which would be
distracting.

Yes, I know I've described the Ticklerton loo in this book,
but that's only for historic record because they aren't like that
nowadays. I don't expound a fictional extravaganza about
how four people at a house-party held a debating society there-
in for twenty-three out of twenty-four hours a day – they'd
have been jolly unpopular with the other five members of the
household if they had. The WC is an essential room in any
establishment, but it is not the *only* room: its actual usage can
be taken for granted. And a public urinal may well be left out
of literature, although it is undoubtedly a public convenience.

Of course, you don't find *women* there. People with a lava-
tory complex are incompatible with love.

Eric certainly liked, and knew a reasonable amount about
women when he was young; but either he had purposely forgotten it, or in his novels he was deliberately manufacturing
puppets. Some of his puppets are carefully and painstakingly
made, but they are not always painted in quite the right colours. Some have a resemblance to women – Dorothy is con-

scientious and hardworking, and Rosemary is rather a nice girl – but they don't *behave* like women. All too clearly, we see the dangling strings.

But do a few improbable characters in the novels matter, when he has given us the unparalleled perfection of *Animal Farm*?

There is relentless humour and inescapable tragedy in *Animal Farm*, where to obey is not to be honoured. There are heroes and villains, where the good come to grief, and the wicked flourish. There is ruthlessness rewarded, and there is trust betrayed, where the wheel turns full circle through the whole parable and paradox of man. It is the most exquisite satire in the English language.

But there are no women in *Animal Farm* : Mrs Jones is barely named before she vanishes from the scene.

And there is no sex.

1: THE SECOND-BIRTHDAY PARTY BABY: Jacintha 1903.

2: EDWARDIAN FAMILY: The Buddicom children Christmas
1907. (l to r) Jacintha, Guinever, Prosper.

3: HOLIDAY AT
NEWQUAY: August
1903. (l to r) Nurse A[...]
(Alice Burnham, later
one of the 'Brides in t[...]
Bath'), Guinever, Jacin[...]
Prosper. Our mother
standing on the upper
step behind us.

4: TEAPARTY ON THE
RIVER: July 1914. The
Hennerton Backwater,
off the Thames. Note the
antique picnic basket,
the teatray and the
wicker-covered milk
bottle. (l to r) Auntie
Mimi, Jacintha, Guinever,
Prosper, Nors, our
mother.

5: OUTSIDE TH[...]
FRONT DOOR A[...]
TICKLERTON:
about 1913 to 19[...]
Prosper on pony
held by Jacintha
the others prob-
lematical. (The
grown-up looks [...]
Miss Auden, so t[...]
two boys may be
little Auden boy[...]
staying with the[...]
Grandfather, the
Rev. Preb. T. Au[...]
who lived at Ch[...]
Stretton. They a[...]
obviously broth[...]
and younger tha[...]
Prosper, then age
or 10.)

IAY-WAIN AT CHARLTON HILL: September 1914. (l to r) Our mother, Jacintha,
ever, Prosper. Charlton Hill, near Wroxeter, was the home of our Great-Aunt
 Jenkins, widow of Admiral Jenkins (descendant of James II and the Naughty
Bagot whose portrait was kept in the place of honour in the upstairs drawing-
 but with her face virtuously turned to the wall – and very cross the unamused
rian Aunt Maria was with our mother when she surreptitiously turned it the right
round to look at the unmentionable Beauty). Charlton Hill was an interesting
, at that time full of treasures: including the Family Coach, last used about 1840
ow so populated by moths and mice that we were not allowed to play in it.

HE WREKIN FROM CHARLTON HILL: 8th September 1914. (l to r) Jacintha,
ever, our mother, Prosper.

8: THE CARRIAGE
WAITING TO TAKE U
TO CHURCH:
CHARLTON HILL 191
The most ordinary
people had Coachmen
with Silk Cockades in
those days. Aunt Marie
carriage-horses were
named Shales and June
The child in its Sunday
best is Guinever.

9: ANOTHER PROBLEM CHILD: about
1914 or 1915. Guiny thinks it might be
herself, but it looks to me more like
Avril.

10: DEFINITELY GUINY AT THE SA
PERIOD: 1914 or 1915. In her car, with
her cat – Mannie of course. (Her face
a different shape from the face in 9.)

11: THE FIRST BLUE PERSIAN
1914. Our mother with Quillie a
Guiny with Mannie, at The Shar

12: THATCHED COTTAGE, SHIPLAKE-ON-THAMES, 1914. *The cottage where we were living when we first met Eric. The field on the far side of the clump of elm trees was where he stood on his head to attract our attention. The steep path through the field was popular when we played bicycle-races.*

BACK DOOR OF THATCHED COTTAGE. It was near this back door that we were playing French Cricket when we met Eric.

14: QUARRY HOUSE, SHIPLAKE-ON-THAMES. *On the other side of the far-distant hedge is the kitchen-garden: then the boundary hedge to ROSE LAWN.*

15: *ROSE LAWN, STATION ROAD, SHIPLAKE-ON-THAMES.* Home of the Blairs when we first met Eric. It has since had some alterations, which are not very apparent in this recent photo.

16: *TICKLERTON COURT, CHURCH STRETTON, SHROPSHIRE.* Home of our grandfather, William Squire Buddicom, as it was in our young day. It was in the wall about 5 feet thick between the drawing and dining rooms, below the chimney, that Eric and I thought there might be a secret room.

17: CROQUET AT TICKLERTON: September 1917.
(l to r) Prosper, Guinever, Eric.

18: IN THE STABLE-YARD AT TICKLERTON: September 1917.
(l to r) Eric, Guinever, Prosper.

19: SHOOTING PARTY AT CHELMICK, TICKLERTON: September 1917. (l to r) Eric, Guiny, Ted Hall (the Ticklerton keeper) Prosper. Guiny has evidently shot the first rabbit of the day.

20: RETURN FROM SHOOTING: THE STABLE-YARD AT TICKLERTON September 1917. (l to r) Prosper, Guiny, Auntie Lilian, Ted Hall, Eric.

21: 'ERIC AND THE GIRLS FISHING' (about 1917). Caption by Prosper to mounted snapshot, presumably taken by himself Guiny and Eric are obvious but the second girl doesn't resemble me and is too old for Avril. Guiny and I think the background looks like the Ticklerton Pool: if so, it might have been one of our Hornby Cousins, Lucy or Georgina, who lived at The Bank House, Ticklerton and might have come to tea. Avril and I were not at Ticklerton with Guiny Prosper, and Eric in 1917

22: *JACINTHA AND JOAN HORNE (about April 1918). By the Yew Walk at ?icklerton. From the bare trees and vernal flora it should be April; and since Joan has her hair up, it cannot be earlier than 1918. The Hornes were another large, party-giving friendly family who lived at The White House, Church Stretton: one of Joan's brothers, Kenneth, was later a constant entertainment in his broadcasts till his untimely death.*

3: *QUARRY HOUSE, WEST GARDEN FRONT The three-light window on the left is in the dining-room — the window through which the boys shot at their hundred-yard target. The room above it the nursery.*

The Pagan.

So here are you, & here am I,
Where we may thank our gods to be;
Above the earth, beneath the sky,
Naked souls, alive & free.
The autumn wind goes rustling by
And stirs the stubble round our feet;
Out of the west it whispering blow
Bringing its earthy odours sweet,
Stops to caress & onward goes.
See with what pride the setting sun
Kinglike in gold & purple dies,
~~So — to shine before our eyes~~
And like a robe of rainbow spun
Tinges the earth with shades divine.
That mystic light is in your eyes
And ever in your heart ~~shall~~ will shine.

28: *INGLE-SEAT ALCOVE IN QUARRY HOUSE DINING-ROOM. Where Jacintha and Quillie were sitting when Eric wrote his sonnet, at the opposite writing-table alcove, January 1919.*

29: *36 ST MARKS ROAD, HENLEY-ON-THAMES: 1972. The Blairs' chief home from 1916 to 1921; looking much the same as it did then.*

30: *PROSPER'S DIARY FOR 1920. Typical page-opening showing frequent companionship of Eric.*

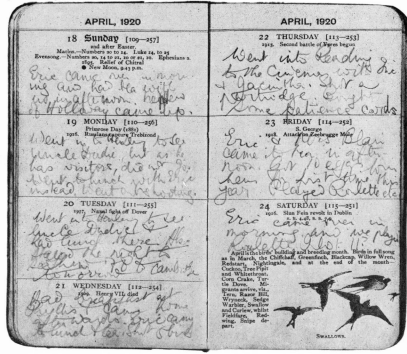

APRIL, 1920

18 Sunday [109—257]
2nd after Easter.
Matins.—Numbers 20 to 14. Luke 14, to 25
Evensong.—Numbers 20, 14 to 21, 20 or 21, 20. Ephesians 2.
1895. Relief of Chitral
New Moon, 9.43 p.m.

Eric came over in morning and had tea with us in afternoon, heaps of Holliday came up.

19 MONDAY [110—256]
Primrose Day (1881)
1916. Russians capture Trebizond

Went up to Henley to see Uncle Dakie, but as he has visitors, did not go. Slept to lunch with Eric instead. Went a bird-hunting.

20 TUESDAY [111—255]
1917. Naval fight off Dover

Went into Henley to see Uncle Dakie's had lunch there. Stayed the night & leaving tomorrow to Cambridge.

21 WEDNESDAY [112—254]
1509. Henry VII died

Bad breakfast got Phyllis came home afterwards. Eric came to lunch & we went birds.

APRIL, 1920

22 THURSDAY [113—253]
1915. Second battle of Ypres begun

Went into Reading to the Cinema with Eric & Jacintha. Shot a partridge. Bought some Patience cards.

23 FRIDAY [114—252]
S. George
1918. Attack on Zeebrugge Mole

Eric & Mrs Blair came to tea in afternoon. Got 70 eggs from hens for first time this year. Played Roulette etc.

24 SATURDAY [115—251]
1916. Sinn Fein revolt in Dublin
S.R. 4.48, S.S. 7.0

Eric came over in morning and we played Roulette got 115

April is the birds' building and breeding month. Birds in full song as in March, the Chiffchaff, Greenfinch, Blackcap, Willow Wren, Redstart, Nightingale, and at the end of the month—Cuckoo, Tree Pipit and Whitethroat, Corn Crake, Turtle Dove. Migrants arrive, viz., Tern, Razor Bill, Wryneck, Sedge Warbler, Swallow and Curlew, whilst Fieldfares, Redwing, Snipe depart.

SWALLOWS.

31: (left) INSCRIPTION BY ERIC IN THE MILTON. Written at Eton before he gave the book to Guiny. August 1921.

32: (Above) ERIC, 1921. This 'Studio portrait' which he gave us is in a slightly different pose from the one at The Orwell Archive.

33: US, 1921. Easter Holiday Daisies at Quarry House. (l to r) Alan, Jacintha, Prosper, Guinever, Nors. With the dog Bobby, afterwards given to Eric when the Blairs were at Southwold.

ETON COLLEGE,
WINDSOR.

27/6/20.

My dear Mrs Buddicome,

You said very
kindly last holidays that I might come
& watch the race at Henley on the 30th from
your punt. Do you still intend going there,
& may I come? I should be very glad if
you could let me know before Wednes-
-day. I am sorry I have given you such
short notice; if you are not going I
shall of course spend the day with my
Father. I should be very glad if you
could tell me where arrange meet to, & where
& when to meet you. I might pick you up at
Shiplake, as my train would pass there about
11.35 or so. I am going to meet Father in Henley.

I hope the weather will be a little better than
it is today or Wednesday.

Yours sincerely,

Eric Blair.

34: LETTER FROM ERIC TO OUR MOTHER: 27 June 1920.
Compare handwriting with 1949 letter: illustrations 36,37

35: BACK PAGE OF LETTER. With turnip caricature of Eric by
himself in pencil below the signature – copied lower down

36: THE LAST LETTER REMAINING
FROM ERIC TO JACINTHA: May
22nd 1949. Compare with 34-35.

37: BACK PAGE OF LETTER.
Signature indecipherable, but handwriting said to be definitely Eric's.

Cranham
Tuesday

Hail and Fare Well, my dear Jacintha,

You see I
haven't forgotten. I wrote to you yesterday but the letter isn't
posted yet, so I'll go on to cheer this dismal day. It's been a day
when everything's gone wrong. First there was a stupid accident to the
book I was reading, which is now unreadable. After that the typewriter
stuck & I'm too poorly to fix it. I've managed to borrow a substitute
but it's not much better. Ever since I got your letter I've been remembering. I can't stop thinking about the young days with you & Guin
& Prosper, & things put out of mind for 20 or 30 years. I am so wanting
to see you. We must meet when I get out of this place, but the doctor
says I'll have to stay another 3 or 4 months.

I would like you to see Richard. He can't read yet & is rather
backward in talking, but he's as keen on fishing as I was & loves working on the farm, where he's really quite helpful. He has an enormous
interest in machinery, which may be useful to him later on. When I was
not much more than his age I always knew I wanted to write, but for the
first ten years it was very hard to make a living. I had to take a lot
of beastly jobs to earn enough to keep going & could only write in any
spare time that was left, when I was too tired& had to destroy a dozen
pages for one that was worth keeping. I tore up a whole novel once &
wish now I hadn't been so ruthless. Parts of it might have been worth
re-writing, though it's impossible to come back to something written
in such a different world. But I am rather sorry now. (" 'An w'en I
sor wot 'e'd bin an' gorn an' done, I sed coo lor, wot 'ave you bin
an' gorn an' done ? ") I think it's rather a good thing Richard is such
an entirely practical child.

Are you fond of children ? I think you must be. You were much a
tender-hearted girl, always full of pity for the creatures we others
shot & killed. But you were not so tender-hearted to me when you abandoned me to Burma with all hope denied. We are older now, & with this
wretched illness the years will have taken more toll of me than of you.
But I am well cared-for here & feel much better than I did when I got
here last month. As soon as I can get back to London I do so want us to
meet again.

As we always ended so that there should be no ending

Farewell and Hail

Eric

38: 'REMEMBERING' LETTER FROM ERIC TO JACINTHA. Tuesday 15th
February 1949. The identifying caption at the top of the page was written
in later by Jacintha.

13

Nineteen Twenty-Two – Nineteen Twenty-Seven: Departure and Return

NINETEEN TWENTY-TWO WAS Eric's last year in England before he went to Burma. By that time the parent Blairs had settled in Southwold, and Eric had left Eton at the end of 1921. So the two families were a good way apart and we did not see very much of him.

Guiny has a *Shakespeare Birthday Book*, inscribed, 'Guin, with much love from Prosper, Xmas 1921', in which the signature *Eric Blair* appears for his birthday, 25 June. The Shakespeare mottoes for that date were:

> *What man didst thou ever know unthrift*
> *that was beloved after his means?*
>   Timon of Athens, Act iv, Sc 3.

> *An you had an eye behind you, you might see more*
> *detraction at your heels than fortunes before you.*
>   Twelfth Night, Act II, Sc 5.

Neither seems very agreeable for his career.

No more of Eric's letters are extant for that year. The chief written data is an account-book of my mother's, whereby we are noted as having taken up residence at Oldfield House on 19 December 1921, with Prosper and Guiny going up to Ticklerton for Christmas, and me by myself in January 1922 for the Shropshire Hunt Balls; that for Easter we returned to Quarry House, where mention is made of Prosper – now nearly eighteen – having acquired a motor-bicycle; and that for the summer holidays the whole family was at Ticklerton.

For most of 1922 we had a rather nice French boy called André staying with us to learn English. He and Guiny were great allies as they were both crazy about Carpentier, the French Boxing Champion, then at the height of his fame. André rigged up some sort of punch-ball for boxing practice, and Eric was certainly at Quarry House with us that April, because we can remember him playing about with this contraption with Prosper and André, who was a year or two older. They also played about with Prosper's new motor-bike. When it was being demonstrated, Eric made some remark to the effect, 'I don't mind so much about *starting* it – I want to know how to *stop* the darn thing.'

I think Eric was still at Shiplake when, towards the end of the holidays, I went up to Ticklerton for a prolonged visit. Grandpapa and Uncle John had died within a few days of each other at the end of February, and Auntie Lilian was lonely by herself. I had my twenty-first birthday-party there, with a fine birthday-cake sent up by my mother. And shortly afterwards, accompanied by Miss Auden, Auntie Lilian took me for a motor-tour of Devon and Cornwall. We went in the Ford, driven by Lewis the then Ticklerton gardener who, like most of the men on the estate, could turn his hand to anything. But he told Guiny, next time he saw her, that the trip had nearly killed him – I suppose because we did such extensive sight-seeing. Auntie Lilian and 'Aunt Nettie' could never decide which of the two beauty spots in a neighbourhood they would like to look at most, so we invariably sampled both.

I was staying with Uncle Dudie for Henley Regatta, and went back to Oldfield House in time for Lord's – to which I think Eric went with us: I am sure we were both at the Eton and Harrow match more than just in 1920 and 1921. For those to whom this function is foreign, it was always the etiquette to wear a flower-favour in the colour of the side you supported: pale blue (a dyed carnation or love-in-a-mist) for Eton, dark blue (constantly a cornflower) for Harrow. I had to *wear* a cornflower – WHAT would Prosper have done if I hadn't, to say nothing of Uncle Wallace – but it always appealed to me very much to be escorted by an Etonian as well as the dark blue Prosper and Co. There were a lot of cornflowers in the Oldfield House garden. I don't know if they were planted on purpose.

Oldfield House had a long garden, with a tennis-court, backing on to the playing-fields. It was while we were surveying these fields once, from the deck-chairs in our garden, that one of the Harrow boys – I think it was Brian Rattigan – told us what we all thought an excellent anecdote typifying the three major English Public Schools:

An Eton boy, a Harrow boy, and a Winchester boy were all standing watching a cricket-match, and a lady was standing beside them. The Eton boy smiled at her politely, raised his cap, and said 'Do let me get you a chair', but made no move to get one. The Winchester boy didn't say a word, but quietly went off and fetched a chair for her. And the Harrow boy sat on it.

Looking back, I thing Eric must have come to stay at least twice on short visits to Oldfield House. I can remember distinctly a conversation taking place in the drawing-room, with him and Tony Michell, one of Prosper's nicest Harrow friends, about Eric's great hero M R James. Dr Montague Rhodes James was Provost of Eton while Eric was there, and it was a very special privilege for some of the older boys to have breakfast with him. Eric was most proud of having achieved this honour when he reached a suitable form for it, and we thought him very fortunate indeed. There was no exact equivalent at Harrow to the unsurpassable M R James at Eton, whose ghost stories we all so admired. Eric was particularly impressed by his style, which was indeed impressive : never an unnecessary word, and unwithered by age. It was, I think, to M R James that the best of Eric's style is owed.

Another memory of Eric at Harrow is of another walk with him, past a particularly attractive house called The Orchard. It was a long walk, and we had a long conversation through the walking.

A long walk was about the only way you could have any sort of private conversation at Oldfield House, which was always full of people. The gregarious Prosper had a good many friends to whom our mother gave a standing invitation, so a lot of boys were always turning up in any spare moments, and especially on Sundays for tea. There was some sort of convention for innumerable doughnuts to be eaten for Sunday tea, so our mother provided them in such vast quantities that however many were consumed, there were always some left over. And the ones left over had to be finished by the family for Monday lunch in a horrible concoction called Doughnut Trifle. In vain I tried to persuade my mother that a trifle should be based on sponge cake, for which, however disguised by raspberry jam, cream, and sherry, the-day-before-yesterday's doughnuts were no substitute : next Monday, Doughnut Trifle would appear again.

When we lived at Harrow, there were boys in and out of the house all the time, so I knew plenty with whom to compare Eric. Before that, when Prosper was at prep school, there were his prep school friends. Some used to come to stay at Shiplake and Ticklerton in the holidays, and when I was at Redmoor, Canford Cliffs – this being near to Branksome Park – Mr and Mrs Phillips, who ran The Old Ride, used to have me to tea there on several Sundays or half-holidays each term 'so that I could see my brother' – and, of course, incidentally, other boys as well. There was another girl at Redmoor with a brother at The Old Ride, who was asked to tea there, too.

We had very few contemporaries at Shiplake, but there were about eight or ten boys in Shropshire we usually saw when we went up there and whom we knew quite well. And among all the boys we knew, Eric was one of the most interesting, the best-informed, the kindest, the *nicest*.

Guiny and I can remember the first day that we met him : Shiplake was such a small village then that a strange indigenous child was as rare as a winged dragon. But neither of us can remember the last time we saw him before he left for Burma. It cannot have been *known* then that it was going to be the last time. I don't think he came to stay at Ticklerton during the 1922 summer holidays, when our whole family, and André, were up there for six or seven weeks : and there was certainly no farewell party at the Docks to which we were invited to see him off, or anything of that sort.

It was in October 1922 that he was exiled to the Burmese Police.

*   *   *   *

He wrote me three letters from Burma. The first was a long one, in the strain 'You could never understand how awful it is if you hadn't been here' – very disconsolate, but unspecific. He didn't explain why and how it was so awful. I replied that if it was as bad as that, hadn't he better leave and come home ? He answered briefly that he *couldn't* leave : and afterwards he wrote at greater length, but it seemed guardedly. I got the impression that perhaps correspondence might be censored.

I did not reply to these last two letters, for which I am very sorry indeed. But it just *happened*, without being deliberate. To begin with, I simply did not know what to say. The solution, 'Come home if it's so unbearable', had already been offered and not well received. The obvious alternative, 'Then I suppose you'll have to put up with it', hardly seemed worth saying. And I had not changed my mind. Before I got round to writing, the letters were lost and I couldn't remember the address. If we'd still been at Shiplake with the Blair family at Rose Lawn, it would have been easy enough, but they were moving from one place to another at Southwold.

The letters were lost because I myself was leading a nomadic life at the time. After Prosper left Harrow, we were mostly at Ticklerton: but I was not very much with my immediate family. Besides Auntie Lilian, there were Auntie Mimi with Noël, and my great-aunt Toddie, all childless, with whom now that I was grown-up I was rather in demand as a 'visiting niece'. With Uncle Dudie too, I used to stay for weeks at a time, as first preference. He was now living entirely at Phyllis in the summer, and often part of the winter as well, when he was not abroad. The food at Phyllis, in those days, was very good indeed: so as I was always a bit of a pig I was quite happy there for a while, sampling new and delicious dishes, and doing a little mild clerical work when necessary, for which he kept me well supplied with pocket money.

And then there was Prosper at Oxford, with his – as usual – numerous Oxford friends, some of whom became my friends as well. Prosper himself and so many contemporaries are gone with the vanishing years: but there are still two or three, with their subsequent wives, with whom I keep up a correspondence, though as we five in different parts of the country we seldom meet nowadays. I am godmother to the daughter of one of them, and their news is usually of further grandchildren.

Prosper enjoyed Oxford very much, and so did Guiny and I, with Eights Weeks, Commem Balls, etc. Prosper, unfortunately, enjoyed it *too* much — he did not start working till his last term, which was leaving it too late.

*   *   *   *

When Eric returned to England in 1927, he spent a fortnight with Auntie Lilian at Ticklerton, where Prosper and Guiny were then staying. But completely unavoidable circumstances prevented me from joining the party. Guiny says that he had 'altered', but does not seem to know exactly how. And Auntie Lilian wrote to me at the time that he was 'very different'.

After that he completely disappeared, and none of us heard a word from him. So we had no idea that he had changed his name.

We may have been a disappointment to him. After the 'awfulness' of Burma, he seems to have taken a burden of care on his shoulders. And he would have grown away from Prosper, who used the precious time at Oxford, that Eric had so longed for, in merely frivolling around, chasing after girls and crawling after pubs and nightclubs, without even achieving a degree.

And I, the one he always talked to, was not there.

14

Nineteen Forty-Nine:
Hail and Farewell

ERIC HAD SLIPPED away without trace after his visit to Ticklerton in 1927. I don't know why I made no attempt to write to him, but I didn't, and he wrote neither to me nor to Prosper. Our mother and Mrs Blair had had occasional correspondence when first the Blairs migrated to Southwold, but after two or three years this had lapsed. Guiny and Avril, though very friendly companions when they were children together, had somehow never taken to writing to each other. So the two families quite lost touch. But we sometimes talked of Eric nostalgically and wondered what had become of him: and I was disappointed that his name never appeared in any List of Authors.

I used to keep a diary: no voluminous affair, just a little pocketbook with a week to a double-page, for a brief account of daily events. After we came down to Bognor, I gave this up – nothing ever happens here – but when I lived in Chelsea, the pages were crammed. Through the War and a few years after, I was working in National Savings and the Ministry of Works, going to Shiplake nearly every weekend to be with my mother, who by then suffered from serious heart trouble. Prosper was in the Army, and married, but Guiny and Nors both took local war jobs, to be able to look after her and gave them up as soon as the war was over. In Chelsea, and other parts of London, for that matter, there must have been a fearfully social life going on — I seemed to be out practically every day and evening to lunch, and tea, and dinner, and innumerable parties. My 1949 diary is typical of this régime, except that in it are included notes of all contact in 1949 with Eric.

From the DIARY (Boots, 4″ x 2½″) :

FEB.	8 Tuesday	Letter from Auntie Lilian saying George Orwell was Eric Blair.
	9 Wednesday	Rang up Martin Secker to find out about Eric and wrote to him.
	11 Friday	To Foyles where I bought another copy of *Animal Farm*. [*To take to my mother at the weekend*.]
	17 Thursday	2 letters from Eric Blair when I got home. [*Presumably by second post*.]
	19 Saturday	To Foyles at lunchtime and bought *Burmese Days*.
MAR.	19 Saturday	Wrote to Eric with messages from O.L. [*The Old Lady, as we called our mother*.]
	27 Sunday	Took them Eric's book on *Paris and London*. [*To Shiplake*.]
APR.	9 Saturday	To Shiplake by 4 pm train. O.L. had another book of Eric's called *Coming up for Air*. [*Probably she had ordered it from Bumpus, where she had a current account and constantly bought books*.]
	24 Sunday	Read *Coming up for Air* to the Old Lady.
MAY	18 Wednesday	Wrote to Eric.
	24 Tuesday	Letter from Eric.
JUNE	2 Thursday	Wrote to Eric.

8 Wednesday   Letter from Eric about 'Nothing ever dies'.
11 Saturday   Only just caught 4 pm without a ticket. Guiny met me in the *Essex*. The Old Lady was on the Porch, looking towards the West, and I had tea with her. Sunny day, but she said she felt cold. She showed me Eric's new book, which is very morbid. She talked a lot about him.

There is no further reference to Eric after 11 June.

*   *   *   *

Auntie Lilian had seen an article in one of the literary weeklies divulging that *George Orwell* was the pen-name of Eric Blair : but it was so long ago, I don't remember which paper. This was the first any of us had heard of his changed identity, and I was enthralled with delight that he had 'made it' after all. The only book by George Orwell I had ever seen was *Animal Farm*, but it had impressed me more than anything I had read for years. Of course, once you knew, it was obvious that it could only have been written by Eric. It was so exactly like him, so exactly the book he would have loved to read if someone else had written it when he was a boy. It is a *beautiful* book.

William Empson (in *Orwell at the B.B.C.*) says that when it first came out, Eric complained of the critics that 'not one of them said it's a beautiful book'. But that is the exact phrase I had always used when talking about it, and what I wrote to Eric, although I did not know what he had said to William Empson. But much to my regret, he never referred to *Animal Farm* in his letters to me : though he made a potent reference to *Nineteen Eighty Four*.

The day after this exciting news came from Auntie Lilian – the Shropshire letters always arrived by the second post, after I'd left for the office, so I couldn't read it till I got home in the evening, too late to do anything that night – first thing next morning I rang up Secker and Warburg, whose name appeared on the title-page of *Animal Farm* as the publishers: to try to contact Eric at once.

But easier said than done. The man they put me on to was helpful and friendly, but he broke it gently that he had disturbing news to impart. He explained that Eric was seriously ill with TB in a sanatorium in Gloucestershire, and gave his address. So I wrote immediately, full of enthusiasm for the glorious *Animal Farm*, and regretful for the state of his health.

A week later I received two letters from him, both together in the same envelope which was postmarked 'Gloucester – A – 12.5 pm 16 Feb 1949'. Both are quite long, typewritten letters. The first of the two is dated '14.2.49', but the second simply 'Tuesday'. February 14th 1949 according to the diary-heading was a Monday: 'St Valentine's Day, Old Candlemas Day'. So the letter headed 'Tuesday', in the envelope postmarked 16 Feb 1949, must have been written on Tuesday, 15 February. The first of these letters is the letter of an old friend catching up with his news after an absence of nearly thirty years: the second, written next day, after further remembering, is far more characteristic – just the sort of letter he used to write me in 'the young days' as he calls them.

(1)   The Cotswold Sanatorium
                                                 Cranham
                                                 Glos.
                                                 14.2.49

Dear Jacintha

How nice to get your letter after all these years. I suppose it must be 30 years since the winter holidays when I stayed with you at Shiplake, though I saw Prosper and Guinever a good deal later, in 1927, when I stayed with them at Ticklerton after coming back from Burma. After that I was living in various parts of the world and often in great difficulties about making a living and I rather lost touch with a lot of old friends. I seem to remember Prosper got married about 1930.

I am a widower. My wife died suddenly four years ago, leaving me with a little (adopted) son who was then not quite a year old. Most of the time since then Avril has been keeping house for me, and we have been living in Jura in the Hebrides, or more properly the Western Isles. I think we are going in any case to keep on the house there, but with my health as it now is I imagine I shall have to spend at least the winters in some get-at-able place where there is a doctor. In any case Richard, my little boy. who will be 5 in May, will soon have to start going to school, which he can't satisfactorily do on the island.

I have been having this dreary disease (T.B.) in an acute way since the autumn of 1947. but of course it has been hanging over me all my life, and actually I think I had my first go of it in early childhood. I spent the first half of 1948 in hospital, then went home much better after being treated with streptomycin, then began to feel ill again about September. I couldn't go for treatment then because I had to finish off a beastly book which, owing to illness, I had been messing about with for eighteen months. So I didn't get to this place till about the beginning of the year, by which time I was rather sorry for myself. I am trying now not to do any work at all, and shan't start for another month or two. All I do is read and do crossword puzzles. I am well looked after here and can keep quiet and warm and not worry about anything, which is about the only treatment that is any good in my opinion. Thank goodness Richard is extremely tough and healthy and is unlikely I should think, ever to get this disease.

I have never been back to the Henley area, except once passing through the town in a car. I wonder what happened to that property your mother had which we used to hunt all over with those 'saloon rifles' and which seemed so enormous in those days. Do you remember our passion for R. Austin Freeman? I have never really lost it, and I think I must have read his entire works except some of the very last ones. I think he only died quite recently, at a great age.

I hope to get out of here in the spring or summer, and if so I shall be in London or near London for a bit. In that case I'll come and look you up if you would like it. Meanwhile if you'd care to write again and tell me some more news I'd be very pleased. I am afraid this is rather a poor letter, but I can't write long letters at present because it tires me to sit up for long at a time.

Yours
Eric Blair

(2)

Cranham
Tuesday

Hail and Fare Well, my dear Jacintha

You see I haven't forgotten. I wrote to you yesterday but the letter isn't posted yet, so I'll go on to cheer this dismal day. It's been a day when everything's gone wrong. First there was a stupid accident to the book I was reading, which is now unreadable. After that the typewriter stuck & I'm too poorly to fix it. I've managed to borrow a substitute but it's not much better. Ever since I got your letter I've been remembering. I can't stop thinking about the young days with you & Guin & Prosper, & things put out of mind for 20 or 30 years. I am so wanting to see you. We must meet when I get out of this place, but the doctor says I'll have to stay another 3 or 4 months.

I would like you to see Richard. He can't read yet & is rather backward in talking, but he's as keen on fishing as I was & loves working on the farm, where he's really quite helpful. He has an enormous interest in machinery, which may be useful to him later on. When I was not much more than his age I always knew I wanted to write, but for the first ten years it was very hard to make a living. I had to take a lot of beastly jobs to earn enough to keep going & could only write in any spare time that was left, when I was too tired & had to destroy a dozen pages for one that was worth keeping. I tore up a whole novel once & wish now I hadn't been so ruthless. Parts of it might have been worth re-writing, though it's impossible to come back to something written in such a different world. But I am rather sorry now. ('An' w'en I sor wot 'e'd bin an' gorn an' done, I sed coo lor, wot 'ave you bin an' gorn an' done?') I think it's rather a good thing Richard is such an entirely practical child.

151

Are you fond of children? I think you must be. You were
such a tender-hearted girl, always full of pity for the creatures
we others shot and killed. But you were not so tender-hearted
to me when you abandoned me to Burma with all hope denied.
We are older now, and with this wretched illness the years will
have taken more toll of me than of you. But I am well cared
for here & feel much better than I did when I got here last
month. As soon as I can get back to London I do so want us
to meet again.

      As we always ended so that there should be no ending
                    Farewell and Hail
                         Eric

This is the old familiar kind of letter he used to write in
those long-ago days when we were at school, except that it
hasn't any poetry quotations or criticism in it – though it *has*
got a bit of criticism of himself, and *one* quotation, even if it
isn't poetry : the old favourite joke from *Punch* that we used
to quote and re-quote to each other on every possible occasion.
The drawing was of a warship readied for the Admiral's inspec-
tion : a sailor had knocked a bucket of tar all over the newly-
scrubbed deck, and another sailor was explaining to the Petty
Officer : 'An' w'en I sor wot e'd bin an' gorn an' done, I sed
coo lor! Wot 'ave you bin an' gorn an' done?' That old joke
alone, together with the ever-constant beginning and ending,
would hallmark that letter as Eric.

The envelope is very pale blue, the right size for quarto
folded into four : the letters are on quarto paper, deep cream
without a watermark. The first occupies one sheet and about a
third of another, the second is one well-filled sheet. Examining
them, the typeface of the second is certainly different from the
first, but it also looks more decrepit, so it's not surprising that
the 'borrowed substitute's not much better'. One other thing
which I have noticed about these two letters, as I was copying them, is that in the first he writes 'and' in full, whereas the

second is all ampersands. *Formality* after a hiatus of many years changing to the *familiarity* of renewed friendship? I think ampersands were his more usual habit – they are in the later handwritten letter of 1949, and in his old 1920-21 letters.

His descriptive touches are tantalising: we wonder *what* book he was reading, and *what* stupid accident rendered it unreadable. My own books are far too frequently unreadable through being dropped in the bath, where I have an inveterate but regrettable custom of reading myself to sleep. They are never quite the same again, even after three days in the airing cupboard. And that second letter of Eric's met the same fate, as I was reading and re-reading it, calling up memories – if not spirits – of our 'young days' from the vasty deep of the sub-conscious, when I began to write a Memoir of him. The bath is a good place for meditation, as well as reading. I am glad he wrote to me 'to cheer that dismal day'. It does seem to have been *one of those days*: I bet it was raining, and that he had stodgy rice-pudding for lunch, made with skim-milk. O Ghost of Tabby.

But I wish now that I had answered it earlier. At the time, I wanted to read some of the hitherto-undiscovered books first, and I started on *Down and Out* – which, although extremely interesting, very much disconcerted me: I could not imagine the Eric I had known embarking on such a life. Next I went on to *Burmese Days*, which I liked, and which seemed impressively well written and mature for a first novel. My diary records that I did not write back till 19 March 'with messages from the Old Lady', while I was at Shiplake for the weekend. My mother was very interested in *Animal Farm*, which she had not read before, and I left *Burmese Days* behind for her that weekend: but I had not broken *Down and Out* to her yet.

She ordered some of his books herself: I have just looked at our copy of *Critical Essays* (2nd impression, May 1946) in which there is a bill from Bumpus, to

Mrs. L. L. Norsworthy, F.R.Hist.S.   23/3/49
   1 Lion & the Unicorn   2.0
   1 Animal Farm   6.0
   1 Critical Essays   8.6
      Postage & Packing   6
                    ——
                   17.0
                    ——

Other books on order to follow.

Prices were certainly more moderate, even in 1949. Imagine three books' *Postage and packing sixpence* (2½p) today – when a second-class letter costs more and can't be guaranteed to get there. To say nothing of the prices of the books themselves. All hardback.

I received no reply to my letter of 19 March: I don't remember what was in it, but it was sympathetic and friendly. Ian Angus says that around that time Eric had had a relapse and was very seriously ill indeed.

But we went on buying, and reading, any of his books we could get hold of, and when I went down to Shiplake at the weekends, my mother and I would discuss our latest acquisitions with increasing bewilderment.

Perhaps it is better to work upwards. Starting with *Animal Farm* set an untowardly high standard. We liked *Burmese Days* and the *Essays*, but since we were neither of us very politically inclined, we were perhaps incapable of properly appreciating *The Road to Wigan Pier* – it seemed a bit patronising and inclined to pull cockroaches rather than plums out of the pie, without much in the way of constructive remedy.

By *Homage to Catalonia* I was shocked. For a journalist to pay homage in a literary exposition is one thing, but to take arms in alien seas of trouble is another. It is impertinence for independent members of a different nationality to interfere with the internal affairs of a country not their own. How would we like it if a couple of chaps from the Kremlin came along and machine-gunned Mr Wilson? Or if a man from Marseilles popped over to take a pot-shot at Mr Heath – bringing his wife with him to carry the sandwiches in case he found the House involved in an all-night sitting?

By the other novels we were more baffled still. There was no question as to the excellence of the writing: Eric had achieved a mastery of his chosen profession which even the 'stern critic' himself could not have faulted. And we found the books extremely interesting, in particular *Coming up for Air* with the recognisable Henley. But it was difficult to correlate their author with Eric.

The Eric we had known had been a philosophical and admirably balanced boy: a boy of sympathetic understanding and withal a sense of humour. But the novels are all frustration. Occasionally a person one might like to meet flitters across a page, but the main characters are so unmercifully fated to failure. Their creator writes as though simple, enduring happiness is not only impossible but also in some way wrong: the dial only counts the shadowed hours.

What had become of his good-humoured cynicism, his infectious – because so tolerant – smile? It is true that life does not give us unadulterated merriment: there is nothing to smile at in desolating grief and high tragedy. But there is no high tragedy and desolating grief in the three novels – nor is there much smiling, either: just petty restriction and eternal disillusionment. If only *one* of them could have had, if not a happy, at least an encouraging ending – the *Aspidistra* isn't really encouraging: we know too well the leopard doesn't change its spots, and that Gordon will bite the next hand that feeds him as sulkily as he bit the last.

And perhaps Eric *doesn't* like women? Look how all the girls end up. Look at Dorothy, still being a *Clergyman's Daughter*, back to the glue and brown paper in the vicarage – and glue you have to boil is as smelly as tramps. Look at Rosemary, stuck with *Keeping the Aspidistra Flying* when she wanted a geranium – and fancy fancying wet-rag Gordon Comstock. Look at Elsie, prevented from *Coming up for Air* because she's suffocated into a 'sagging bulldog', a 'shuffling old woman', *at only forty-seven*. Can you credit it?

About the middle of May, my mother commented that it was some time since I had heard anything of Eric, so on 18 May I wrote again, to ask if he would like any books or jigsaw puzzles, and got a reply on the 24th:

> CRANHAM LODGE
> CRANHAM
> GLOUCESTER
> 22.5.49

Dear Jacintha

Thanks so much for your letter. I'd have written before, but I've been most horribly ill & am not very grand now. I can't write much of a letter because it tires me to sit up. Thanks awfully for the offer, but I'm generally pretty well supplied with books & things. It looks as if I am going to be in bed for months yet. I have sent for my little boy to come & stay with friends nearby. I think he'll like it, & as he is now 5 he can perhaps start going to day school. I hope to see you when I am in town if I ever am.

Yrs
[*completely indecipherable signature – looks like E I*]

This letter is on a single sheet of pale blue notepaper, with the address as a printed heading, and additional printed information 'TELEGRAMS: "HOFFMAN, BIRDLIP" and TELEPHONE: WITCOMBE 2195' in the opposite corner. The envelope, in matching colour, is the same kind as the previous one, and postmarked 'GLOUCESTER – A – 7.15 pm 23 May 1949'.

When I received it, I did not think it was from Eric – that is to say most certainly not *written* by him, since the writing (it is all handwritten including the envelope) is entirely different from his old handwriting which I knew so well indeed. I imagined that, because he had been so 'horribly ill', he was not well enough to write himself and that he had dictated it to a nurse or somebody at the sanatorium. But when in 1971 I took it up to London University Library to show to the Keeper of the *Orwell Archive*, Ian Angus, he assured me that it *was* Eric's own latter-day handwriting and exhibited other samples in proof.

Masters of graphology might find it interesting to compare Eric's old and new selves by a study of the two different hands.

I answered this letter on 2 June, and he replied on 8 June. There seems to be a fate against Eric's letters. I am sorry this one was lost too, because it was the last I had from him, and was important though brief. My diary records: 'Letter from Eric about Nothing Ever Dies.'

As I remember, it was in the same handwriting on another sheet of the same addressed paper, and it defined his faith in some sort of after-life. Not necessarily, or even probably, a conventional Heaven-or-Hell, but the firm belief that 'nothing ever dies', that we must go on *somewhere*. And it ended, with our old ending, *Farewell and Hail*. He probably wrote it because I had told him that my mother was ill: though I had not stressed this unduly, since he was in such poor health himself.

As usual, I went down to Shiplake the next Saturday, 11 June, when my mother 'showed me Eric's new book, which is very morbid. She talked a lot about him.' Bumpus had been forewarned to send her a copy of Eric's projected work as soon as it was published. It was a sunny day, and she was lying on the garden chaise-longue on the porch, covered with a rug although it was so warm, and looking very frail. I sat beside her, in the western sunshine with a long, cool 'pirate's drink' of rum and orange with a lot of soda-water, while she reminisced about Eric with affection, as a boy. She dwelt on the remembrance of his unfulfilled wish to go to Oxford, wondering whether there was anything she could have said or done to make old Mr Blair change his mind : and grieving for the might-have-been if he had not perforce gone out to Burma. She had been very fond of Eric, and the defeatist destruction of all individuality portrayed by him in the nightmare world of *Nineteen Eighty Four* upset her very much. So when I left her on the Sunday evening, I left with her his letter declaring that *nothing ever dies* – to comfort her that perhaps he would have better luck next time. I never saw that letter again.

And I never saw my mother again. She had a last, fatal heart attack in the early hours of Tuesday morning, 14 June : and they telephoned to me in Chelsea to tell me she was dead.

Nineteen Eighty Four is inextricably tied up in my mind with my mother's death. Eric had described it to me as 'a beastly book', which – since he struggled against time to go on writing it when he was utterly unfit to do so – to all intents and purposes killed him. It would be unreasonable to imagine that it also killed my mother : but she was very frail indeed when she read it, and it certainly did not make any happier her last few days of life.

So I never answered his final lost letter. And seven months later we learned from the newspapers that Eric himself was dead. I took the long, typewritten Hail-and-Farewell letter from its companion in its envelope, and folded it round the crucifix he had given me to keep me safe from Dracula : and the two stayed together, as belonging to each other, in my jewel-box.

*   *   *

Leaving undone the things we ought to have done is sometimes worse than doing the things we ought not to have done. Too many years too late, at Christmas 1971, I sang him a little song : it was called *FIFTY YEARS ON* :

Dear ghost, forgive –
I can't explain
rejected
vow,
neglected
pen –
if I could live
my life again
would I do now
as I did then?

Most possibly I would.

But I very much regret *now* that I never made any attempt to see him when he was so ill in Gloucester. And I don't know *now* why I didn't. He said in all his letters that he wanted to see me, so surely I could have gone up there just for one week-end? But it never occurred to me: all his letters suggested his meeting me when he returned to London, not my going to Cranham to see him. And I never thought of it myself.

Fortunately the young and beautiful Sonia Brownell took a much more realistic view of the proper treatment for invalids, so she *did* take the trouble to make the journey. And married him so that she would be better able to look after him. I am most heartfeltly glad that for his last weeks of life, in hospital, he had the comforting promise of happiness in a shared future with her, and the knowledge that his work was now being given overwhelming recognition.

But it is so very sad that he had no time left for the promise to be fulfilled: that after all his years of anxious poverty and disappointment 'finding it very hard to make a living', the final fame and fortune, and the hope of happiness, all came too late.

Twenty years after his death, he is a more *Famous Author* than ever 'which nobody can deny'. The imaginary *Collected Editions* are all there, in substance, on the bookshelves; together with translations into more languages than ever occurred to

our most optimistic dreams. The films and the television programmes we could not have thought of: but what an excitement they would have been to the young Eric, if he had known.

Nineteen Eighty Four was a book that changed the direction
of the world. In waking us all up to the dangers of the Totali-
tarian State, its value is supreme. True, the tail may now be
wagging the dog, and it is questionable whether it is any better
to have unwilling strikers *forced* to strike, causing untold
havoc and wrecking the economy of the country. But the warn-
ing has been given, and the danger has been shown – whatever
particular Brother may take it upon himself to be Big Brother.
And with *absolute* freedom for *everybody*, who indeed is truly
free?

It is really from sheer personal prejudice that I so love
Animal Farm and so hate *Nineteen Eighty Four*. In *Animal
Farm* I should have been all right: I would obviously have been
The Cat, invariably absent at the appropriate moment, so I
should have got on very well. In *Nineteen Eighty Four* I
shouldn't have lasted ten minutes: mine would have been one
of the first heads to roll – and a good thing too. A million times
better to be dead instantaneously, in that intolerable world.

But I wish that Eric were still here, with two or three more
books to his credit. Books that were neither the working-off of
shoulder-chips such as the novels, nor yet political treatises
for which he has said the first and last political words. But
books about *people*: the sort of people we would like to know.
People who, although they must meet with misfortunes as part
of the reality of life, do sometimes have *nice* things happening
to them as well. And, as the extra walnut on top of the cake,
at long last his long-ago promised Book of Ghost Stories.

I wish that Eric were still here, now that I am already and
he would be also, seventy, so that after all the years – even
if it wasn't by our own united fireside – we could still say to
each other, 'Do you remember?'

The Envoy

EX MEMORIAM

So rhymes and runes are cast once more:
Reflecting through the written page
We trace beyond death's distant door
The dream days of our golden age.
Some foreprint of a master-plan
With children other children share –
The child is father to the man –
George Orwell once was Eric Blair.

Notes

ERIC ALWAYS WROTE me pages of notes on any book or poem that interested him, so here are a few to keep up the tradition.

AVE ATQUE VALE:

This bit of Catallus was one of his favourites, and *Hail and Farewell* we adopted as our private salutation, ending *Farewell and Hail*, so that we should meet again.

As many rhymes as are reasonable end in 'l' because there are bells running through the song (like Chopin with Notre Dame) but the word 'bell' is carefully *not mentioned*. *Quail* in the first verse is a forerunner of the hopeful bell of the *'ail'* words in the second: and *O Infidel* in the second verse is an echo of the tolling bell for the *'el'* words in the first.

THE ULTIMATE BRITANNIAN: Eric himself is an example of a Britannian (an un-dictionary word he invented himself in the First World War). It is more than just a *Briton*: it is a *Rule Britannian*, convinced we never *shall* be slaves, because an Englishman never knows when he's beaten, and after winning the Battle of Waterloo on the Playing Fields of Eton, an Englishman's home is his castle, so when in Rome do as Ramsgate does, etc., *ad lib.*

SHADOWS CHILL: remembrance of the poem he wrote me at Rickmansworth.

O INFIDEL: An apostrophisation we got out of some forgotten book, which we often used to each other, e.g. once when Mrs Blair wasn't going to be at home, on the maid's day out, she gave us 3d to buy something at the baker's for tea. You got a lot of things for ½d each or 7 for 3d in those days. Eric suggested currant buns, but I wanted crumpets 'because they're nice toasted with butter'. Eric replied: 'Then you have never tasted toasted buttered buns, and in penance for my superior knowledge, I shall toast and butter them *for* you, O Infidel.' Every line could have notes, but we need not be excessive, and a prose paraphrase might run:

> Hello Eric, you were an awfully nice boy and I'm sorry you disappeared. Little did we know what was in store. I agree that *Nineteen Eighty Four* was a beastly book that killed you, but it has been useful in waking people up to discourage the sands of the Sahara and the Siberian Steppes from surging into Shakespeare's England.
>
> You blazed the trail, now firmly fixed for successors far beyond Winston Smith. But pull your socks up. There is more to life than unmitigated gloom. God has seen it all so often before, but he remains unscathed. We have been given hearts for courage and kindness, and the will to be masters of our own fate. The circle has no end.

EX MEMORIAM

The opposite of *In Memoriam* because it is remembrance of things past and long ago venturing OUT. It is a jigsaw puzzle of some of our favourite literature.

RHYMES were among others *Ruthless Rhymes for Heartless Homes* by Harry Graham. Eric could recite nearly all of them, and often did.

RUNES were from *Casting the Runes* by M. R. James. We could never decide whether that, or *Whistle and I'll come to You*, was his masterpiece.

REFLECTING THROUGH: We preferred the *Looking Glass* to *Wonderland* by Lewis Carroll.

DEATH'S DISTANT DOOR: Wells' *Door in the Wall*, "the most haunting title" which Eric very much regretted had been used already.

DREAM DAYS and THE GOLDEN AGE: by Kenneth Grahame,

which had greater appeal for us than the popular *Wind in the Willows*.

THE CHILD IS FATHER TO THE MAN: Yes, I know it should be "of", and I know it is *The Rainbow*: nevertheless, parts of Wordsworth's *Intimations of Immortality* we thought magnificent.

Lines 5 and 6: Congenial children don't need to pretend with each other. They have no axes to grind, no states to keep up, no reason to be anything but themselves.

FOREPRINT or PAWPRINT are interchangeable. It is extraordinary that *Foreprint*, the only exact word that meets the situation, does not seem to be in the dictionary. If I'm not allowed foreprint, then I'll have pawprint: but *Foreprint* is what I mean, much as I love *paws*.

Lines 7 and 8: He grew up to be eventually, after or in spite of the various vicissitudes, very much the man you might have expected.

THE HOUSES

I have described the various houses we lived in in some detail, because they are no longer as they used to be.

THE THATCHED COTTAGE, where we first met Eric, and Burwood Glen, Gran Finlay's house at Bournemouth, have been pulled down altogether and other things built up instead.

TREVONE, Uncle Dudie's house at Shiplake, he himself had altered and enlarged in the late 1930's, rechristening it Bolney Trevor. It is now more conventional, with kitchen premises, dining-room, sitting-room and study downstairs, and upstairs four bedrooms each with its own private bathroom, plus two smaller bedrooms that have to share a bathroom between them. Within the last few years, all the orchards and the north field have been sold for building-plots, and there are now ten or a dozen houses where there once was one.

TICKLERTON COURT, Grandpapa Buddicom's home in Shropshire, has had the entire top storey taken off, and the two north rooms of each floor removed as well. So the nurseries, the museum-room, the huge laundry-attic, the haunted bedroom, and the maids' rooms – as well as the attics proper in the roof – no longer exist. The rooms that Prosper and I used to sleep in – the end north rooms on the first floor, his the east-windowed one and mine the west – are gone now, as are the kitchens and store-rooms below. I am told that the conversion has been extremely skilfully done, 'you wouldn't know it had ever been anything different': but though I have several times visited Shropshire since Prosper sold everything he could of the estate, I have never had the heart to look at the house.

QUARRY HOUSE, our childhoods' home that my father built at Shiplake, I *did* look at after the new owner had altered it – and I wish I hadn't. All the '*art nouveau*' features, the built-in dining-room alcove, and the in-and-outness of the sitting-rooms have been removed: it is now just oblong boxes. The Robin's south window from the porch went away when the porch was incorporated with the drawing-room to square it up. And the lovely wistaria we used to have on the west wall of the house, and the peach tree on the south, are not there any more. *Tempus fugit* indeed: with the guests too, now star-scattered.

BLAIR

CHARLES BLA[...]
b 1743   d 1802
of Winterborne Whitechurch, Do[...]
Owner of "Estates, plantati[...]
messuages, hereditaments[...]
slaves in the Island of Jama[...]

| several | children who mostly died youn[...] |

CHARLES
of Whatcombe, Dorset

| several children | one of the youngest was |

REV. THOMAS RICHARD ARTHUR = FRANCES
b 1802 at Ensbury, Dorset. d 1865
Retired from Colonial Service in the
Church to become Vicar of Milborne St.
Andrew, Dorset, in 1854

(FANNY) HA[...]
whose parents
lived at the Co[...]
of Good Hop[...]
She married [...]
after her eld[...]
jilted T.R.A[...]

| Ten children: Eight died before 1908: one "HOEY" living in New Zealand later | The youngest was |

RICHARD WALMESLEY B[...]
(MR BLAIR)

b. 7 Jan 1857   d. 28 June 19[...]
at Milborne St. Andrew.

Sub-deputy Agent in Opium
Department of Government of In[...]
1875-1912. Secretary of Golf Cl[...]
Harpeden after retirement.

MARJORIE
b 21 April 1898
in Bengal.
d 3 May 1946
m. July 1920
HUMPHREY DAKIN
(b 1895, d 25 Nov. 1970)
Leaving children

EILEEN O'SHAUNESSY ① = E[...]
m. 9 June 1936
d. 29 March 1945
aged 39

(G[...]
b 2[...]
Ber[...]

RICHARD H[...]
(adopted s[...]
b. 14 May [...]

DY MARY FANE
41
daughter of Thomas,
Earl of Westmorland: a
y of playwrights, composers,
s. and diplomats.

G. E. LIMOUZIN
b. in France.
Shipowner and Teak Merchant
in Moulmein, Burma.

[among other children]

FRANK = ②THERESA
b at Limoges. d 1915   HALLILAY
Teak Merchant in Moulmein   b in England. d 1925
Burma, where a street is   Family Matriarch in
named after the Limoozin   Burma
family

Nine children, including in England

MABEL LIMOUZIN   NELLIE   CHARLES   GEORGE
                      lived in   Sec. of Golf club   m. IVY
MRS BLAIR)   Portobello Rd   at Parkstone,
                      and afterwards   Bournemouth
ay 1875 } d. 19 March 1943   in Paris
e, Surrey }   m. M. ADAN

UR = ②SONIA BROWNELL   AVRIL NORA
    m 13 October 1949   b. 6 April 1908
tahari   at Henley-on-Thames
n 1950   m. WILLIAM DUNN

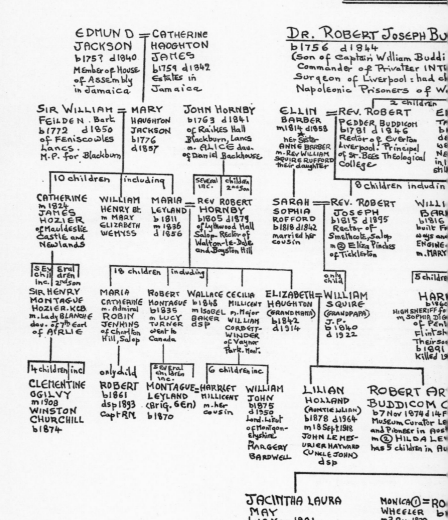

BUDDIC[...]

EDMUND JACKSON b175? d1840 Member of House of Assembly in Jamaica = **CATHERINE HAUGHTON JAMES** b1759 d1842 Estates in Jamaica

DR. ROBERT JOSEPH BU[...] b1756 d1844 (Son of Captain William Buddi[...] Commander of Privateer INTE[...] Surgeon of Liverpool: had ch[...] Napoleonic Prisoners of W[...]

SIR WILLIAM FEILDEN. Bart b1772 d1850 of Feniscowles Lancs. M.P. for Blackburn = **MARY HAUGHTON JACKSON** b1776 d1857

JOHN HORNBY b1763 d1841 of Raikes Hall Blackburn, Lancs. m. ALICE dau. of Daniel Backhouse

ELLIN BARBER m1814 d1858 her sister ANNE BARBER m. REV WILLIAM SQUIRE RUFFORD their daughter = **REV. ROBERT PEDDER BUDDICOM** b1781 d1846 Rector of Everton Liverpool: Principal of St. Bees Theological College

E[...] TA[...] b[...] de[...] we[...] NE[...] in[...] sti[...]

2 children

10 children including

CATHERINE m 1824 **JAMES HOZIER** of Mauldeslie Castle and Newlands

WILLIAM HENRY Bt. m MARY ELIZABETH WEMYSS

MARIA LEYLAND b1811 m 1836 d 1856

REV ROBERT HORNBY b1805 d1879 of Lythwood Hall Salop. Rector of Walton-le-Dale and Bayston Hill

SARAH SOPHIA ROFFORD b1818 d1842 married her cousin = **REV. ROBERT JOSEPH** b1815 d1895 Rector of Smethcote, Salop m② Eliza Pinches of Ticklerton

WILLI[...] BARN[...] b1816 built F[...] ways an[...] ENGINE[...] m. MARY

Several children inc. 2nd son

8 children includin[...]

5 childre[...]

Several children Inc. 2nd son **SIR HENRY MONTAGUE HOZIER. K.C.B.** m. Lady BLANCHE dau. of 7th Earl of AIRLIE

18 children including

MARIA CATHERINE m. Admiral ROBIN JENKINS of Charlton Hill, Salop

ROBERT MONTAGUE b1835 m LUCY TURNER went to Canada

WALLACE b1848 m ISOBEL BAKER dsp

CECILIA MILLICENT m. Major WILLIAM CORBETT-WINDER of Vaynor Park, Mont.

ELIZABETH HAUGHTON (GRANDMAMA) b1842 d1914 = **WILLIAM SQUIRE (GRANDPAPA)** J.P. b1840 d 1922

only child

HAR[...] b186[...] High Sheriff fo[...] m Sophia Di[...] of Pen[...] Flintsh[...] Their son[...] b1891 Killed 19[...]

4 children inc. **CLEMENTINE OGILVY** m1908 WINSTON CHURCHILL b1874

only child **ROBERT** b1861 dsp1893 CaptRN

Several children inc. **MONTAGUE LEYLAND (Brig. Gen)** b1870

HARRIET MILLICENT m. her cousin

6 children inc.

WILLIAM JOHN b1875 d1950 Lord. Lieut of Montgomeryshire m MARGERY BARDWELL

LILIAN HOLLAND (AUNTIE LILIAN) b1878 d1964 m 18 Sept 1918 JOHN LE MESURIER HAYWARD (UNCLE JOHN) dsp

ROBERT AR[...] BUDDICOM [...] b 7 Nov 1874 d 14 F[...] Museum Curator Le[...] and Pioneer in Aus[...] m② HILDA LE[...] has 5 children in Au[...]

JACINTHA LAURA MAY b 10 May 1901

MONICA① = RO[...] WHEELER b[...] m 3 Aug 1929

MILY TREE

⌐NCES. PEDDER

⌐way marriage 1780
⌐ter of Robert Pedder
⌐ney, and Jane Tarleton.)

					EDMUND(?) = Mrs "LUCIE" SHANLEY

EDMUND(?) = Mrs "LUCIE" SHANLEY
WHEATLEY   one of the BEAUTIFUL
of Mirfield   MISS MARSDENS OF BATH
Yorkshire   she escaped from the
died young   French Revolution on a
in France   Pass signed by Robespierre
              with her two little boys

⌐ENRY	ALICE = CHARLES	WILLIAM	2 boys HENRY EDMUND =	ELIZA
⌐ d1854	TOWNSEND GEDYE	FINLAY	WHEATLEY	BROOKES

⌐ENRY
⌐NTLE
⌐6 d1854

⌐IZA
⌐GILL

ALICE = CHARLES
TOWNSEND GEDYE
b1798
Son of JOHN
GEDYE of St.
Neots, Cornwall
b1770—and
ANNIE DANGAR
settled in Australia

WILLIAM
FINLAY
wrote poetry
m.. MARY
MILLER
(grand-daughter
of 5th Duke of
Argyll)
both died young

2 boys
HENRY EDMUND =
WHEATLEY
b1792 d1841
Fought at
Waterloo

ELIZA
BROOKES
m 1820
niece of
JOSHUA BROOKES
Anatomist
(1761—1833)

⌐ren inc   5 Children including   5 children inc   6 children   including

⌐MARY = CHARLES TOWNSEND	ALEXANDER = ELIZABETH	CORNELIA	MALVINA

⌐MARY = CHARLES TOWNSEND
⌐ARRIET GEDYE (GREENIE)
⌐834   b1833 d 1900
⌐876   of Dangar, Gedye
⌐nited & Malloch: Sydney
⌐stralian N.S.W.
⌐tercolours

ALEXANDER = ELIZABETH
LAWRENCE   LUCIE
Professor of   b1820
Languages at   d after 1904
Glasgow
University

CORNELIA
MARY
b1826
m SELLER
went out to
America

MALVINA
FRANCOISE
ROSALIE
b1828
m . W·K.
DAVIES

⌐daughters born   in Australia   7 children   including

⌐NCE	MADELEINE	LAURA = REGINALD	ADELINE	EDITH	ARTHUR	ALYS

⌐NCE
⌐Y
⌐d1910
⌐OR
⌐GE

MADELEINE
ALICE
(TODDIE)
b1856 d1934
m. EDWARD
LOVELL-CLARE
dsp

LAURA = REGINALD
MARY   EDMUND
(GRAN)   ALEXANDER
b1854 d1933 (GRANNIFATHER)
         b1846 d1906
         a great
         traveller

ADELINE
LUCIE
dsp
unmarried

EDITH
ELIZA
m
McCULLOCH

ARTHUR
WILLIAM
m
AUGUSTA
dsp

ALYS
ELLEN
m
EDWARD
MAYNARD
GOSLETT
of Gosletts
in Charing X
Road.

⌐   4 children born   in Australia

⌐ LUCIE	MILDRED	REGINALD	ALAN	BERTRAM	GORDON

⌐ LUCIE
⌐Y (MITS)
⌐7 d 14 JUNE 1949
⌐DERICK WILLIAM
⌐THY (NORS)
⌐ d1 Aug 1960

MILDRED
ETHEL
(AUNTIE MIMI)
b1879 d1960
m 3 Feb 1913
Dr. NOEL
BURKE

REGINALD
GEDYE
(UNCLE DUDIE)
b1881 d1952
dsp
unmarried

ALAN
GORDON
b1891 d1959
m
FLORENCE
GALLAGHER

BERTRAM
McCULLOCH
m
WILLS

GORDON
GOSLETT
m
MABEL
WALLIS

⌐R GEDYE = ② CYNTHIA   GUINEVER LAURA
⌐3 March 1968   ARUNDEL   OLIVIA NORSWORTHY
              m 26 Sept 1936   b 3 February 1907

⌐ENNIFER = SIMON BROWN
⌐7 June 1937   b 9 April 1937
              Barrister